BALANCING
THE BANKS

BALANCING
THE BANKS

Global Lessons from the Financial Crisis

MATHIAS DEWATRIPONT, JEAN-CHARLES ROCHET,
AND JEAN TIROLE

Translated by Keith Tribe

Princeton University Press
Princeton and Oxford

Copyright © 2010 by Princeton University Press

Published by Princeton University Press,
41 William Street, Princeton, New Jersey 08540
In the United Kingdom: Princeton University Press,
6 Oxford Street, Woodstock, Oxfordshire OX20 1TW
press.princeton.edu

Library of Congress Cataloging-in-Publication Data

Dewatripont, M. (Mathias)
  Balancing the banks : global lessons from the financial crisis / Mathias
Dewatripont, Jean-Charles Rochet, and Jean Tirole ; translated by Keith Tribe.
    p. cm.
  Includes bibliographical references and index.
  ISBN 978-0-691-14523-5 (hbk. : alk. paper) 1. Banks and banking—
Government policy. 2. Banks and banking—State supervision. 3. Global
Financial Crisis, 2008–2009. 4. Financial crises—History—21st century.
  I. Rochet, Jean-Charles. II. Tirole, Jean. III. Tribe, Keith. IV. Title.
  HG1573.D49 2010
  332.1—dc22   2009052389

British Library Cataloging-in-Publication Data is available

This book has been composed in Sabon
Printed on acid-free paper. ∞
Printed in the United States of America
10 9 8 7 6 5 4 3 2

Contents

Acknowledgments

JEAN TIROLE thanks Nicolas Chanut, Frédéric Cherbonnier, Jacques Delpla, Mathias Dewatripont, Pierre-Olivier Gourinchas, Marc Ivaldi, Jean-Pierre Landau, Sylvie Matherat, Michel Pébereau, Jean-Charles Rochet, Philippe Trainar, and participants at various conferences and seminars for very useful discussions and comments. The author is also very grateful to Keith Tribe for translating chapter 2 from French, and to Richard Baggaley for very helpful suggestions.

Jean-Charles Rochet thanks Charles Calomiris, Patrick Honohan, Rafael Repullo, and all those who attended several seminars at the Banque de France, the Bank of Canada, and the Central Bank of Brazil, especially Sylvie Matherat and Eduardo Lundberg. He has also profited from detailed comments made by Jean Tirole on a draft version of his chapter. Responsibility for the arguments advanced here lie solely with the author, of course.

Mathias Dewatripont and Jean-Charles Rochet thank Janet Mitchell and Peter Praet.

Chapter 2 by Jean Tirole was first published as "Leçons d'une crise," *Toulouse School of Economics Notes* no. 1 12/2008 (online at www.tse-fr.eu/images/TSE/TSENotes/notes%281%29j.tirole%28pdf%29.pdf).

Chapter 3 by Jean-Charles Rochet was first published as "Le futur de la réglementation bancaire," *Toulouse School of Economics Notes* no. 2 12/2008 (online at www.tse-fr.eu/images/TSE/TSENotes/notes%282%29rochet%28pdf%29.pdf).

Chapter 4 by Mathias Dewatripont and Jean-Charles Rochet, "The Treatment of Distressed Banks," first appeared as a chapter of an electronic book by CEPR and Vox, entitled *Financial Regulation and Macroeconomic Stability: Key Issues for the G20* (edited by Mathias Dewatripont, Xavier Freixas, and Richard Portes; see http://www.voxeu.org/reports/G20_ebook.pdf). It was prepared for a meeting held in London on January 31, 2009.

BALANCING
THE BANKS

CHAPTER 1

Introduction

Mathias Dewatripont, Jean-Charles Rochet,
and Jean Tirole

THE RECENT FINANCIAL crisis was a mix of "unique" and much more conventional events. This short book offers our perspective on what happened and especially on the lessons to be learned in order to avoid a repetition of this large-scale meltdown of financial markets, industrial recession, and public deficits. Chapter 2 provides a diagnosis of what went wrong and discusses some key financial regulation reforms. Chapter 3 takes a more detailed look at the flaws in the prudential framework that was in place when the crisis erupted and at the required remedies, and chapter 4 focuses on the treatment of distressed banks, a key element of this prudential framework. This introduction takes a more general look at the rationale for and challenges of banking regulation.

REGULATION IN A HISTORICAL PERSPECTIVE

What degree of regulation of the banking sector is appropriate has been a controversial question for almost a century. The Great Depression, with its wave of bank failures triggered by bank runs, led in the 1930s to heavy-handed regulation, combining deposit insurance, interest-rate regulations, barriers to entry, restrictions on activities (compulsory specialization), and constraints on bank size. Although the succeeding decades witnessed a return to stability, the banking system gradually became perceived as inefficient and poorly innovative. In order to encourage cost-cutting and innovation, and to induce banks to pass efficiency gains on to consumers, governments deregulated the banking industry and fostered competition from the 1970s on. This trend was also the result of pressure from commercial banks, which were facing competition from other less regulated financial institutions (e.g., money-market mutual funds and investment banks).

Although details vary from country to country, the removal of interest-rate controls promoted competition at first. In the turbulent macroeconomic environment of the 1970s and 1980s, though, this form of deregulation, together with an interest-rate maturity mismatch in a period of rising interest rates, resulted in the 1980s in a large-scale banking crisis in the United States (the savings and loan—S&L—crisis). This crisis led to a mix of further deregulation and reregulation. On the one hand, diversification of activities was allowed in order to reduce the specialization-induced fragility of the S&Ls. S&Ls had used short-term savings deposits to fund long-term, fixed-rate mortgages, and were thereby exposed to yield-curve risk. On the other hand, in order to limit the exposure of deposit insurance funds, the regulation of solvency ratios became more stringent and intervention rules in case of violation of these ratios were strengthened.

This emphasis on prudential regulation and the desire to harmonize country-specific capital adequacy requirements led to the international standard embodied in the Basel system of regulation. New international regulations, including the 1988 accords, were intended to ensure a level playing field in a world of increasing globalization of banking. Subsequent events made this attempt to establish a level playing field, however imperfect in practice, seem prescient since large international banks have now become common in the United States, Europe, and Asia.

This internationalization and the intensification of competition among various marketplaces (e.g., between Wall Street and the City of London) led to a weakening of regulatory standards, fed by pressure from large banks, themselves facing competition from more lightly regulated financial institutions. One can interpret the recent modification of the Basel capital adequacy rules (Basel II), which allow large banks to reduce effective capital ratios if they can show that their risks are "limited," as an outcome of lobbying by these banks. The assessment of risk under the new regulations comes from the banks themselves, through "internal models"—which represents a step toward self-regulation. The complexity of these internal models can make it very hard for supervisors to verify what is being computed and raises concern, despite the requirement that those models be authorized by regulatory authorities.

The trend toward weaker regulation also came from the inability of the system to cope with the pace of financial innovation, itself fed by a desire to lower the amount of capital required by the regulatory agencies. Indeed, the growth of the shadow banking system, of securitization, and of structured products (backed by credit ratings that had been inflated by the rating agencies) can be partly traced to this desire.

The gradual lowering of regulatory standards predated the recent crisis. To be sure, other developments such as "irrational exuberance," loose monetary policy, and global macroeconomic imbalances also contributed to the crisis. But underregulation or ineffective regulation is rightly blamed for playing a central role in the crisis. Not surprisingly, this has led to calls for a strengthening of regulations in a number of countries. It is worth pausing, however, to ask what the purpose and extent of regulation should be.

TO REGULATE OR NOT TO REGULATE?

Banking is one of a handful of industries (others include insurance, financial market making, and pension-fund investing) subject to prudential regulation on top of consumer protection. The focus of this book will be on the former, and more substantial and decisive, form of regulation. This is not to imply that insufficient consumer protection played no role in the recent crisis. Indeed, the crisis started with problems in subprime loans. Although these problems were small compared to the overall crisis that ensued, subprime lending was the release mechanism. Subprime loans are associated with weak consumer protection regulation of banking products in the United States. Therefore the creation of an agency specifically dedicated to strengthening borrower protection in the United States is a welcome development.

What is so unique about banks as to warrant industry-specific regulation? Banks fulfill a specific role in the economy through their involvement in the payment/deposit system as well as in lending to households and firms (for a survey of models of banking, see Freixas and Rochet 2008). Although these activities are essential to the economy, they are no more essential than, say, cars or pharmaceuticals, sectors in which consumer protection regulation exists but not prudential regulation.

In banking, by contrast, prudential regulation has been in place since the 1930s. One classical rationale for such regulation is the vulnerability of individual banks to depositor runs. When wholesale and uninsured retail depositors lose confidence in a bank, their natural reaction is to withdraw their money from the bank as fast as possible. Such bank runs stem from the banks' transformation activity. Banks create liquidity by borrowing short and lending long. By allowing depositors to withdraw their money whenever they feel like it, banks are exposed to self-fulfilling rational panics: as shown by Diamond and Dybvig (1983), when one expects other depositors to run and thereby force the bank into costly asset liquidation, one's dominant strategy becomes to run too. The regulator's monitoring of the institution's leverage (and now liquidity) positions is meant to reduce the frequency of such costly runs.

The recent crisis (as well as some previous episodes, such as the failure of the Long-Term Capital Management hedge fund) has shown that another, related rationale for subjecting the banking industry to prudential regulation could be that the failure of one bank can trigger the failure of other banks through interbank exposures or banking panics. Prudential regulation of banks—in the form of capital ratio requirements plus deposit insurance—is therefore warranted, especially for institutions that are large and interconnected and thus can generate domino effects. In contrast with nonfinancial firms, which are bound to benefit when a competitor goes under, banks can be hurt both as creditors of the failed bank and also as victims of panics that follow a neighbor's insolvency. Prudential regulation is therefore meant to protect the banking infrastructure, the financial system that allows the economy to function smoothly. This warrants that specific attention be paid to large banks.

Yet smaller and not necessarily interconnected banks, whose failure has no systemic consequences, are also subject to prudential regulation. The main reason for this is that their debtholders are small and lacking in monitoring expertise. Deposit insurance is typically introduced in order to reduce the risk that depositors will behave erratically, but it further reduces depositors' incentive to monitor banks.

This rationale for prudential regulation—the lack of expertise and the wastefulness associated with monitoring of balance sheets by retail depositors—explains why prudential regulation is also observed for other institutions with small, dispersed debtholders such as insurance companies and pension funds. Dewatripont and Tirole (1994) discuss in detail the specifics of these institutions and their differences from other financial and nonfinancial institutions that are much more lightly regulated. They formulate the *representation hypothesis*, according to which prudential regulation should aim at replicating the corporate governance of nonfinancial firms, that is, at acting as a representative of the debtholders of banks, insurance companies, and pension funds.

The financial industry has recently substantially increased the magnitude of its "wholesale" liabilities, that is, liabilities held not by small depositors but by other financial institutions. Does this mean that the case for regulation has been weakened? In fact not, because such liabilities, which are often short term and therefore subject to panics, create systemic problems of two sorts: (1) they imply risks for the institution's insured depositors (a case in point is Northern Rock; see the discussion in chapter 3), and (2) even if the institution does not have formally insured deposits (as in the case of investment banks or hedge funds), its failure could create domino effects because of its high degree of interconnectedness with other financial firms (as was the case, for example, with the investment bank Lehman Brothers). Consequently, the argument behind the representation hypothesis still holds: even if the debtholders of banks are neither small nor inexperienced, the fact that their deposits are short term means that when they expect trouble, running is the best strategy. The danger of a bank run for the banking system as a whole then typically prompts the authorities to support endangered institutions. The expectation of this "too big to fail" or "too interconnected to fail" syndrome does prevent panics but it also makes the bank's debtholders passive and creates the potential for excessive risk-taking, in turn implying the need for a debtholder representative to ensure discipline. The social cost of the Lehman Brothers bankruptcy has, if anything, reinforced this argument, since one can now safely expect big banking institutions to be rescued in case of financial distress.

The Challenges Facing Prudential Regulation

According to the representation hypothesis, regulation should mimic the role played by creditors in nonfinancial firms. Since debt gives its owners the right to take control of their borrowers' assets in bad times, regulators must take control of banks in bad times in order to limit the losses of depositors or of the deposit insurance fund. This, in turn, implies the necessity of (1) defining what "bad times" means, and (2) making sure that one can intervene in those circumstances. This is no easy task, even when trouble hits only a single institution; we discuss this case first, and then turn to the more complicated case of multi-institution hardship prompted by negative macroeconomic shocks.

For a single institution, bad times are defined as times at which its capital falls below the regulatory solvency ratio, as defined by the Basel I and II international agreements. Such definitions, although increasingly complex over time, nonetheless yield only rough approximations of a bank's riskiness; for example, they concentrate only on credit risk, and do not fully take into account portfolio risk. Moreover, even in "normal" times, it is a challenging task for the regulator to intervene early enough, given that there is always an "accounting lag" in the computation of solvency. Moreover, this challenge is exacerbated by the fact that, in contrast to nonfinancial firms, banks can take advantage of (explicit or implicit) deposit insurance and "hide" problems of insolvency by aggressively raising money through higher interest rates, a strategy that has been called "gambling for resurrection."

"Market discipline" can to some extent be relied on to help provide early warning signals of a bank's trouble. This can work, however, only if some of the bank's debt is not explicitly or implicitly insured by the state (otherwise its risk premium is zero) or if it is privately insured, so that its insurance premium would reflect market perceptions of its riskiness. Such market discipline can in fact precipitate a crisis by making it more expensive for a bank in trouble to remain insured, and it does not make public intervention in bad times less essential; put differently, market discipline can be only a complement to, not a substitute for, public intervention.

Prompt intervention in an individual insolvency is not straight-forward, but it is even harder in the case of generalized insolvency resulting from a macroeconomic shock. Indeed, multiple factors make taking control of banks during a banking crisis much more complicated. First, banks can expect some sympathy from politicians when they argue that the responsibility is not theirs but instead that of poor macroeconomic conditions. Second, politicians may quickly be faced with a drained deposit insurance fund and be very reluctant to request money from taxpayers to cover the cost of intervention. Third, competent staff from regulatory authorities are likely to be overwhelmed by the sudden magnitude of the task of overseeing multiple interconnected distressed financial firms at once.

In such cases, the temptation to manage the accounts of banks so as to pretend that they are not really insolvent is strong. Such forbearance has been practiced in various crises (e.g., the S&L crisis of the 1980s) but it is dangerous: insolvent banks do misbehave (gambling for resurrection was rampant among S&Ls, for example) and experience shows that the cost to the taxpayer, though delayed, is magnified in the end by such cover-ups. History tells us that, when a crisis hits, honest and speedy cleanups of bank balance sheets are highly desirable: real money is required; accounting tricks won't do. A striking example is provided by the contrast between the Scandinavian and Japanese crises of the 1990s: Japan's procrastination led to years of sluggish GDP growth while Scandinavia "bit the bullet" and came back to satisfactory growth much more quickly.

Building an Adaptive Regulatory System in a Global World

One problem with regulation in recent years is that it has faced accelerating financial innovation. Of course, financial innovation is driven not just by the desire to serve customers better: it can be the result of pure regulatory arbitrage rather than an attempt to increase social surplus (think of structured products with originators keeping senior tranches in order to minimize capital requirements and providing huge off-balance-sheet, and therefore low-capital-requirement, liquidity support to the conduits). More generally, one can expect regulatory arbitrage by the industry (as in the case of rating agencies offering consulting services to boost the ratings of hard-to-understand structured products).

As a consequence, when drafting regulation, legislators should explicitly start from the assumption that these factors will be at play, and they should be willing to adapt the system without delay to these developments. This has, unfortunately, not been the case: regulation is too often designed to "fight the previous crisis" rather than the next one, and is typically one step behind market developments. The trend toward global banking has exacerbated regulation's lag behind market developments.

Indeed, as stressed earlier, recent years have witnessed two significant trends: bigger financial institutions on the domestic scene (with many domestic mergers) and accelerating globalization (partly due to cross-border mergers). On the one hand, these trends have significantly increased the domestic lobbying power of financial institutions, thereby giving more prominence to a laissez-faire approach. On the other hand, globalization in a world of hard-to-coordinate international regulatory policies has increased the lag between private-sector developments and regulatory responses. Taken together, these factors led to Basel II regulatory rules that were less demanding than their predecessors in terms of capital and that even started delegating bits of the actual implementation of supervision to private-sector actors, namely rating agencies or even the (big) banks themselves.

Keeping a Balance

The previous trend toward decreasing capital requirements and increasing delegation of oversight to banks and credit-rating agencies clearly requires a correction, namely a strengthening of regulation. In the recent crisis, the pendulum can be expected to swing in this direction. In such complex industries, however, there are many challenges on the road to efficient regulation.

The first challenge is the need to avoid overreaction: regulation should mimic for banks the corporate governance of nonfinancial firms, not "punish" banks just in order to place blame for the crisis. Although financial institutions that are not yet regulated should be regulated if the regulated sector has large exposures to them (for example, if they are systemically important owing to their large volume of over-the-counter trades with the regulated sector), and although capital ratios should be raised in comparison to precrisis levels, it is much less clear that one should, for example, become prescriptive in terms of business models in banking: the crisis has hit some small as well as some large banks, some private as well as some state-owned banks, and some specialized as well as some universal banks.

The second challenge is the need for politicians to avoid the temptation to be especially harsh in their treatment of banks that have received a bailout—for example, by limiting their ability to pay managers in comparison to their competitors. This can be counterproductive because it means putting them at a competitive disadvantage toward those banks that have not been bailed out, at least *directly* (but that may nonetheless have been *indirect* beneficiaries of bailouts, as creditors of bailed-out banks). By contrast, it does make sense to promote compensation schemes that incentivize bank managers to take a long-term perspective.

Finally, a danger of the recent crisis is that cross-border banking might collapse. This problem, which would be less dire for some large countries such as the United States, is of first-order importance for European countries and some emerging markets. It is linked to the fact that bailout money originates from national treasuries—which are responsible to national electorates—and not from an internationally coordinated insurance fund. Therefore, it is not a surprise that bailed-out banks have in many cases been ordered to favor domestic lending. This trend can mean the end of the European Union's Single Market in banking, which is bad news for the Single Market in general, and therefore for economic growth and efficiency.

The challenges, thus, are numerous. The three essays in this volume discuss a number of principles to deal with these challenges, addressing the microeconomic incentives of financial institutions, the impact of macroeconomic shocks, and the role of political constraints.

CHAPTER 2

Lessons from the Crisis

Jean Tirole

THIS CHAPTER aims to contribute to the debate on financial system reform. In the first part I describe what I perceive to be a massive regulatory failure, a breakdown that goes all the way from regulatory fundamentals to prudential implementation. Although there has been some truly shocking behavior in the world of finance, the universal denunciation of "financial madness" is pointless. Managers and employees in the financial industry, like all economic agents, react to the information and incentives with which they are presented. Bad incentives and bad information generate bad behavior. Accordingly, this chapter starts by listing the principal factors that led to the crisis. Although many excellent and detailed diagnoses are now available,[1] the first section

[1] A particularly readable one is the interesting compendium of contributions by NYU economists edited by Acharya and Richardson (2009). More concise and very useful treatments include the introductory chapter of that book as well as Hellwig (2009).

Of course, this review is bound to become dated with respect to rapidly changing events, new proposals, and meetings of one sort or another. For example, this chapter was completed before the December 2009 Basel club of regulators' proposal of a new solvency and liquidity regime that would deemphasize banks' internal models of risk assessment, force them to hoard enough liquidity to withstand a 30-day freeze in credit markets and to reduce their maturity mismatch, and prohibit those banks with capital close to the minimum required from distributing dividends. The chapter was also completed before President Obama's January 21, 2010, announcement of (among other things) his desire to ban retail banks from engaging in propriety trading (running their own trading desks and owning, investing, or sponsoring hedge funds and private equity groups). More generally, Part I makes no attempt at providing an exhaustive account of the crisis or of the various reform proposals that followed it.

I think it fair to say, however, that the underlying policy issues and fundamental tensions, as discussed in the second part of my chapter and in the rest of the book, will not change so quickly. For example, a G20 meeting or two is not going to remove the problem of maturity mismatches or solve the problem of the exposure of the regulated sphere to the unregulated.

reflects my own interpretation and is therefore key to understanding the policy conclusions I present later.

Many policy makers have forgotten that effective regulation is needed for healthy competition in financial markets, that economic agents should be held accountable for their actions, and that institutions and incentives should lead to a convergence of private and public interests. Although recent events do offer an opportunity for a thorough overhaul of international financial regulation, it is important to strike a balance, showing appropriate political resolve while avoiding the danger of politically motivated reforms in a highly technical domain. The second part of this chapter discusses some implications of recent events for financial-sector regulation.

PART I: WHAT HAPPENED?

The crisis, originating in the U.S. home loans market, quickly spread to other markets, sectors, and countries. The hasty sale of assets at fire-sale prices, a hitherto unprecedented aversion to risk, and the freezing of interbank, bond, and derivatives markets revealed a shortage of high-quality collateral. Starting on August 9, 2007, when the Federal Reserve (Fed) and the European Central Bank (ECB) first intervened in response to the collapse of the interbank market, public intervention reached unprecedented levels. Few anticipated on that day that many similar interventions would follow, that authorities in various countries would have to bail out entire sectors of the banking system, that the bailout of some of the very largest investment banks, a major international insurance company, and two huge government-sponsored companies guaranteeing mortgage loans would cost the American taxpayer hundreds of billions of dollars. A little more than a year later, in the autumn of 2008, the American government had already committed 50 percent of U.S. GDP to its remedial efforts.[2]

---

[2] In mid-November 2008, Bloomberg estimated that $7,400 billion, an amount equal to 50 percent of U.S. GDP, had been guaranteed, lent, or spent by the Fed, the U.S. Treasury, and other federal agencies. On September 2, 2009, the Federal Reserve had $2,107 billion in various assets (including mortgage-backed securities, commercial paper loans, and direct loans to AIG and banks), the Treasury $248.8 billion in Troubled Asset Relief Program (TARP) investments in banks

Equally unforeseen was that American and European governments would find themselves lending significant sums directly to industrial companies to save them from bankruptcy.

Although the crisis has macroeconomic consequences in terms of an immediate and severe recession and of a sharp increase in public debt,[3] this chapter is concerned with financial regulation. Policy makers and economists must have a clear understanding of what happened in order to suggest ways out of the crisis, and especially to propose reforms that will fend off future crises of a similar nature. The proper application of standard economics would in some areas have surely allowed us to steer clear of many obvious errors; and yet the crisis provides us with prima facie evidence on how regulations are designed and evaded, and scope for new thinking about our financial system.

The recent financial crisis will quickly become a central case study for university courses on information and incentives. The losses on the American subprime mortgage market,[4] although significant, were very small relative to the world economy and by themselves could not account for the ensuing "subprime crisis." In other words, the subprime market meltdown was just a detonator for what followed, namely a sequence of incentives and market failures exacerbated by bad news. At each stage in the chain of risk transfers, asymmetric information between contracting parties hampered proper market functioning.

Nonetheless, market failures related to asymmetric information are a permanent feature of financial markets, so the crisis cannot be explained simply in terms of market failures. Two other factors played a critical role. First, a blend of inappropriate and poorly implemented regulation, mainly in the United States but also in Europe, gave individual actors incentives to take sizable

---

and AIG, and the Federal Deposit Insurance Corporation (FDIC) $386 billion in bank debt guarantees and loss-share agreements (source: *Wall Street Journal* Europe edition).

[3] Budget deficits have reached levels unprecedented in peacetime; the steep rise in indebtedness of Western governments will limit room for maneuver in the medium term. Sovereign debt crises might even emerge in member countries of the Organization for Economic Cooperation and Development (OECD), a contingency that was rather remote before the crisis.

[4] Around $1,000 billion, or only 4 percent of the market capitalization of the New York Stock Exchange at the end of 2006 ($25,000 billion), according to the November 2008 estimates of the International Monetary Fund (IMF).

risks, with a major portion of these risks ultimately borne by taxpayers and investors. Second, market and regulatory failures would never have had such an impact if excess liquidity had not encouraged risk-taking behavior.

A Political Resolution to Favor Real Estate

The U.S. administration, Congress, and other officials, including some at the Fed, were eager to promote the acquisition of homes by households.[5] In addition to the incentive for purchasing a home provided by the long-standing and generous tax deductibility of interest paid on mortgages, households were encouraged to lever up their debt in order to acquire homes.[6] Consumer protection was weak, to say the least. Many subprime borrowers were given low "teaser" rates for two or three years, with rates skyrocketing thereafter. They were told that real estate prices would continue to increase and therefore they would be able to refinance their mortgages. Similarly, mortgages indexed to market interest rates (adjustable-rate mortgages, ARMs), which raise obvious concerns about borrowers' ability to make larger payments when interest rates rise, were promoted in times of low interest rates.[7] Alan Greenspan himself called for an increase in the proportion of ARMs.[8]

---

[5] Fortunately, this was not the case in the euro area, where the ECB followed a more stringent monetary policy and authorities in a number of countries did not encourage subprime loans. Of course, loose monetary policy is only a contributing factor, as can be seen from the examples of Australia and Great Britain, two countries where the mortgage market boomed in spite of relatively normal interest rates.

[6] There are several very good outlines of the excesses linked to the housing market—see, for example, Calomiris (2008), Shiller (2009), and Tett (2009).

[7] France has for the most part been spared this phenomenon. French banks have traditionally lent to solvent households, a practice reinforced by law (the Cour de Cassation ruled against a financial institution that had failed in its duty of care by granting a loan incommensurate with the borrower's present or future capacity to repay). Variable-rate loans have always played a relatively minor role in France (24 percent of outstanding loans in 2007), and completely flexible loans, where neither interest rates nor monthly payments are capped, have always had a very small market share (less than 10 percent). Adjustable-rate mortgages are, by contrast, very popular in Spain, the United Kingdom, and Greece.

[8] According to *USA Today* (February 23, 2004), "While borrowers can refinance fixed-rate mortgages, Greenspan said homeowners were paying as much as

Finally, public policy encouraged institutions to lend to subprime borrowers through several channels. Fannie Mae and Freddie Mac were pushed to increase the size of their balance sheets. And loose regulatory treatment of securitization and mortgage-backed securities helped make mortgage claims more liquid.

In response to these policy and social trends, subprime lending changed in nature. Before the first decade of the twenty-first century, lenders would carefully assess whether subprime borrowers were likely to repay their loans. By contrast, recent subprime lending involved an explosion of loans without documentation. For instance, lenders were able to base their calculations on claimed, rather than actual, income. We will return to these developments.

Not surprisingly, U.S. homeownership rose over the period 1997–2005 for all regions and for all age, racial, and income groups. The fraction of owner-occupied homes increased by 11.5 percent over this period. Housing prices moved up nine years in a row, and across the entire United States.[9]

The rise was particularly spectacular for low-income groups. Correspondingly, real estate price indexes in the lowest price tier showed the biggest increases until 2006 and the biggest drop afterward.

Excessive Liquidity, the Savings Glut, and the Housing Bubble

Crises usually find their origin in the lack of discipline that prevails in good times. Macroeconomic factors provided a favorable context for financial institutions to take full advantage of the breaches created by market and regulatory failure. In addition to the political support for real estate ownership, there are several reasons why the origin of the crisis was located in the United States:

0.5 to 1.2 percentage points for that right and the protection against a potential rate rise, which could increase annual after-tax payments by several thousand dollars. He said a Fed study suggested many homeowners could have saved tens of thousands of dollars in the last decade if they had ARMs." Adjustable-rate mortgages made up 28 percent of mortgages in January 2004 in the United States.

[9] These data are taken from Shiller (2009, 5, 36).

A SAVINGS GLUT—EXPANDING THE SET OF BORROWERS
AND REDUCING MARGINS ON CONFORMING LOANS

A strength of the U.S. financial system is that it creates large numbers of tradable securities, that is, stores of value that can easily be acquired and sold by investors trying to adapt to the lack of synchronicity between cash receipts and cash needs. The large volume of securities in the United States was attractive to investors in other countries seeking new investment opportunities and unable to find sufficient amounts of stores of value at home. Surpluses in the sovereign wealth funds of oil-producing and Asian states and the foreign-exchange reserves of countries, such as China, that were enjoying export-led growth built on an undervalued currency, tended to gravitate to the United States. This cash inflow reduced the available volume of stores of value within the United States, and the net increase in the demand for securities stimulated an accelerated securitization of debt so as to create new stores of value that were greatly in demand.[10] Thus, the international savings glut contributed to the increase in securitization that will be described shortly.

Abundant liquidity in the United States led financial institutions to search for new borrowers. They extended their activity in the segment of "nonconforming" or "subprime" loans, that is, loans that do not conform to the high lending standards used by the federal-government-backed Fannie Mae and Freddie Mac. But the enhanced competition associated with excess liquidity also eroded margins made on loans to safer borrowers. This implied that the losses incurred on subprime loans could not be offset by high margins on more traditional lending.

LOOSE MONETARY POLICY

The very low short- and long-term interest rates that prevailed for several years in the early 2000s (for instance, a negative Fed funds real rate from October 2002 through April 2005) made

---

[10] This argument was developed in particular by Caballero, Farhi, and Gourinchas (2008a, 2008b). Ben Bernanke has often pointed to the excess of international savings as the cause of excess liquidity in the U.S. economy before the subprime mortgage crisis.

borrowing extremely cheap. Low short-term rates sow the seeds of a potential crisis through multiple channels:

First, they lower the overall cost of capital and thereby encourage leverage.

Second, they make short-term borrowing relatively cheap compared to long-term borrowing, and therefore encourage maturity mismatches. Low short-term rates thus make for bigger and less liquid balance sheets.

Third, low short-term rates signal the central bank's willingness to sustain such rates, and therefore suggest that, were a crisis to come, the central bank would lower rates and facilitate refinancing, making illiquid balance sheets less costly for financial institutions.

ASSET PRICE BUBBLE

The crisis has revived the debate over the proper attitude of monetary authorities to an asset market-price boom. The stance of central banks in general, and of Alan Greenspan in particular, has been that their remit is limited to inflation and growth, and does not include the stabilization of asset prices, at least insofar as these do not form an inflationary threat. Ben Bernanke, for instance, argued in a series of influential articles[11] that (a) it is usually hard to identify a bubble,[12] and (b) bursting a bubble may well trigger a recession.[13] An auxiliary debate has focused on how authorities should burst a bubble, assuming they have identified one and are willing to risk a recession. It is by no means clear that monetary policy, which controls only short-term rates, is the appropriate instrument. Regulation (by controlling the flow of credit to the bubble market) and fiscal policy (by issuing pub-

---

[11] See, for example, Bernanke (2000).

[12] To take a recent example, one can ask whether the extensive implicit subsidy of mortgages (through fiscal policy, through the government's implicit backing of Fannie Mae and Freddie Mac, and through very low minimum capital requirements for liquidity support granted to vehicles resulting from securitization) did not inflate the perception of mortgage "fundamentals." Ben Bernanke himself in 2005 viewed the unprecedented housing price levels as reflecting strong economic fundamentals rather than a bubble (Tett 2009, 122).

[13] See, e.g., Farhi and Tirole (2010) for a theoretical treatment of the impact of asset price bubbles and their crashes on economic activity.

lic debt and raising interest rates) seem to have a better chance of terminating a bubble.

The alternative[14] to bursting a bubble lies in the government accumulating reserves in advance of such a breakdown. When a bubble ends abruptly, losses are suffered both in the financial and real sectors of the economy, and countercyclical policy becomes necessary. For countercyclical policy to have sufficient room for maneuver, however, governments must have followed conservative fiscal policies during the upswing of the cycle, so as to be able to effectively counter the downswing.

In the debate on the opportunity to stabilize asset prices, it is also important to remember that not only does the extent of the bubble need to be identified, but also who is involved in it. The dotcom bubble at the end of the 1990s created only a very moderate recession when it burst in 2001 because the securities were held mainly by individual households. By contrast, in the recent crisis, heavy losses have been suffered by a broad range of leveraged financial intermediaries, creating widespread problems of liquidity and of solvency.

Robert Shiller, an early and strong proponent of the view that the real estate market exhibited a bubble, has proposed that the short-selling of real estate be made easier, to facilitate stabilizing speculation by those who realize that a bubble is under way.

OMINOUS SIGNALS

The unfolding of the crisis is now well known. Macroeconomic developments led to the stagnation of house prices in 2006; prices in overheated housing markets such as Florida and California stalled; the Fed, which had decreased short-term interest rates from 2000 through 2004 (the Fed funds rate[15] went from 6.50 percent in May 2000 to 1 percent, until June 30, 2004, when it started moving up again), started raising them again (the Fed funds rate was 5.25 percent in September 2007).

In 2006–2007, Chicago Mercantile Exchange housing futures markets predicted large declines in home prices as market participants started worrying about defaults by subprime borrowers.

[14] Proposed by Ricardo Caballero in particular.
[15] This is the rate at which banks lend available funds (reserves at the Fed) to each other overnight.

It was feared that many households whose variable loans were about to reset at higher interest rates would not be able to afford the new terms as stagnating prices made refinancing impossible. Others would go into "strategic default" and not repay their loans when they would go into negative equity (with mortgage balances larger than the total value of their homes).

Although the concerns were very real, it was hard to put clear figures on the magnitude of likely losses. The lag between the signing of a contract and the transition to a higher variable rate, as well as traditional lags associated with downward movements in the housing market, created a real financial time bomb. Furthermore, the cost of borrower default for lenders (including administrative costs, the physical deterioration of vacated homes, taxes, unpaid insurance, realtors' commissions, and falling housing prices) is highly sensitive to the rate of decline in housing prices and other macroeconomic developments. For example, J. P. Morgan estimated in January 2008 that for a decrease of 15 percent in house prices the losses arising from the default of an average "Alt-A adjustable-rate mortgage"[16] taken out in 2006 would be around 45 percent.[17] Another reason why losses are difficult to forecast is uncertainty about public policy, as the rate of unrecovered debt also depends on the level of government assistance.[18]

---

[16] Alt-A mortgages have a risk profile between "prime" and "subprime" loans. For example, the borrower has never defaulted, but the borrowing involves a high level of debt and quite possibly incomplete documentation of financial standing.

[17] Cited by Calomiris (2008, 23).

[18] The FDIC proposed subsidizing a revision of loan conditions, temporarily reducing the rate of interest to be paid by the borrower, and possibly extending the loan term beyond the standard thirty years. Under current law, it is by contrast much more difficult to reduce the principal repayable by the borrower because no such renegotiation can be done without the endorsement of those holding the debt collateralized by the mortgage loan during the process of securitization. The FDIC proposed that the government should underwrite the losses suffered by lenders provided, among other conditions, that the renegotiation resulted in the borrowers' not spending more than 31 percent of their income on mortgage payments.

Excessive Securitization

Although lenders had traditionally retained the bulk of their loans on their own balance sheets, more recently the underlying assets (the repayment of interest and principal on mortgages) were transferred to financial intermediaries, or off-balance-sheet "structured investment vehicles" or "conduits." These intermediate structures were financed mostly through short-term borrowing (say, through commercial paper with an average maturity of about one month). A key innovation was the use of "tranching," as the revenues attached to these structures were divided into different risk classes to suit the needs of different investors. For example, some investors, for risk management or for regulatory reasons, have a high demand for safe AAA securities.[19] Others do not mind taking on more risk.

The rate of securitization of housing loans grew from 30 percent in 1995 to 80 percent in 2006. More tellingly, in the case of the subprime loans the securitized proportion went from 46 percent in 2001 to 81 percent in 2006.

Securitization is a long-established practice, with clear rationales:

First, it allows loan providers to refinance themselves. With the resulting cash, they can then finance other activities in the economy—securitization therefore transforms "dead capital" into "live capital," to use De Soto's (2000) terminology.

Second, when stores of value are in scarce net supply in the economy, the creation of new securities fulfills a demand; this incentive to create new securities in reaction to the savings glut, as we have argued, played a role in the recent increase in securitization.

Finally, in those cases where risks are heavily concentrated, securitization also allows lenders to diversify and spread risk.

Securitization however, shifts responsibility away from the lender, whose incentive to control the quality of its lending is reduced if

---

[19] For detailed accounts of the securitization process, see, e.g., Franke and Krahnen (2008), Brunnermeier (2009), and Tett (2009).

it will not suffer the consequences.[20] The lender may make marginal loans and then divest itself via securitization, without the buyers being able to detect the lack of due diligence. In fact, the rate of default on housing loans of broadly similar characteristics, but differentiated by whether they can easily be securitized or not, can increase by 20 percent according to some estimates when securitization is an option.[21]

This fundamental tension between the creation of liquid assets and incentives to monitor loan quality has two corollaries. First, the lender should not completely disengage itself and should retain part of the risk, as is done, for instance, by insurance companies when they transfer part of their risk to reinsurers. Second, securitization should be linked to certification, a process obligatory for gaining market access and found in other institutions (for example, initial public offerings). Certification should involve a rigorous scrutiny on the part of buyers and rating agencies.

These two principles have not always been followed in the recent crisis. First, the practice of securitization took off at a point when loans became riskier and therefore highly susceptible to informational asymmetries, whereas theory and good practice would dictate that banks should then retain a greater proportion. Lending banks, contrary to tradition, divested themselves of junior (risky) tranches, sometimes in response to the requirements of the prevailing regulatory framework.[22] A number of institutions (such as AIG, UBS, Merrill Lynch, and Citigroup) started sitting on a vast position of the so-called super-senior debt, which they either held directly or insured.

Second, buyers of these securitized loans made their purchases without paying much attention to their quality. Presumably, the fact that the loans were not retained by the original lender should have given the buyers a hint of the likely quality of these loans. But buyers had little incentive to monitor the quality of what

---

[20] Incentive effects and the dangers of securitization have been extensively discussed in the economic literature; see, e.g., Dewatripont and Tirole (1994).

[21] See Keys et al. (forthcoming).

[22] For example, for commercial banks, prudential rules require that 8 percent of assets (weighted by risk) be covered by equity. For triple A tranches, risk is estimated at merely 20 percent, so only 1.6 cents of equity capital is required for each dollar of such assets.

they were buying, in part because favorable credit ratings translate into low capital requirements. Because leverage is the key to profitability, not to mention (for financiers who are heavily ego-driven) the prospect of being at the top of league tables,[23] any risk that buyers were taking by buying these securitized assets was compensated by an opportunity to increase the size of their balance sheets.

Some readers may say that banks, on the whole, kept substantial exposure to the vehicles that they had created. But as we shall see later, they pledged large amounts of liquidity support in case the vehicles had trouble refinancing on the wholesale markets. But that risk was primarily macroeconomic in nature, while the incentives to monitor loans should have been preserved by keeping more of the microeconomic risk!

The Laxity of Credit-Rating Agencies

Credit-rating agencies are once again under fire.[24] In their defense, a foreshortened historical perspective has hindered proper appreciation of the risks linked with newly introduced instruments such as collateralized debt obligation (CDO) tranches or credit-default swaps. Furthermore, the weakness of the macroeconomic treatment in the agencies' models and the departure of personnel lured by clients contributed to poor risk assessment. Yet the failure of rating agencies to fulfill their duties is obvious.

A number of incentive misalignments have repeatedly been pointed out by critics:

- The agencies provided preliminary evaluations (prerating assessments) that allowed lenders to form an idea of what their eventual rating would be, harming transparency.[25]

---

[23] League tables rank the leaders in various areas of banking.

[24] Credit-rating agencies have been criticized before, for instance after the sovereign debt crises of the 1990s and after the bursting of the Internet bubble, both of which they failed to foresee. They reacted very slowly to the problems of Enron, WorldCom, and other companies that failed in 2001.

[25] Such services were requested by lenders, which also did not hesitate to engage in "ratings shopping" for the most favorable rating. Calomiris (2008) notes that Congress, as well as the Securities and Exchange Commission, encouraged ratings inflation.

- In addition, the agencies explained to issuers how they should structure their tranches to barely secure a given rating, say AAA. Even if laxity had been absent, this one practice implied that an AAA tranche carried a probability of default higher than that of AAA securities that had not been the subject of such advice. The activity of credit-rating agencies in explaining how the threshold might be minimally passed rendered the composition of such tranches marginal rather than average.
- The incentives faced by rating agencies seem to have been somewhat perverse, with the commissions paid to agencies being proportional to the value of the issue, therefore generating pressure toward overrating.[26] Rating agencies would normally balance the gains from being easy on issuers against a loss of reputation which would reduce the credibility of their ratings among investors and therefore make agencies less attractive to issuers in the future.
- The desire to please investment banks providing an important percentage of their turnover (structured finance products represented a fraction of close to half of the rating agencies' revenue at the end of the boom) no doubt had a bad influence.
- Finally, the ratings market is very concentrated. There are only three large agencies, and two of them (Moody's and Standard and Poor's) share 80 percent of the market. Where a dual rating is required, these agencies find themselves in a quasi-monopoly situation.

An Excessive Maturity Transformation

A GIGANTIC MATURITY MISMATCH . . .

One essential feature of banking intermediation has always been maturity transformation. The banking system as a whole transforms short-term borrowing from depositors into long-term

---

[26] In June 2008, the three top rating agencies signed a pact with New York's attorney general. Under the old fee system, the agencies had a financial incentive to assign high ratings because they received fees only if a deal was completed; under the new agreement, by contrast, the rating agencies receive payments for service even if a deal is not completed (source: Reuters).

loans to firms. As has long been recognized, this maturity transformation creates hazards for the financial sector. If short-term borrowing is not rolled over, then the banks' liquidity dries up, and the banking system finds itself in trouble. This is especially the case if the bank's creditors panic and seek to withdraw their deposits for fear that the bank might become insolvent. Such panics have now practically vanished for small depositors covered by deposit insurance, but they remain an issue in wholesale finance. Moreover, even if there is no panic, a rise in the short-term interest rate has immediate repercussions for the cost of funds for the financial institution, upsetting its balance sheet.[27]

Recently a number of financial intermediaries—banks and nonbanks—have taken substantial risks by borrowing at very short maturities in wholesale markets (Fed funds market, commercial paper). This strategy is very profitable when the rate of interest is low, but it exposes the financial institution to a rise in the interest rate. The leading commercial-bank illustration of this risk is Northern Rock, whose collapse proved to be very costly for the British taxpayer. The details of this banking panic have been discussed at length in newspapers[28] (for the first time since the 19th century a British bank suffered a run on its retail deposits), but the more fundamental problem was Northern Rock's loss of access to wholesale markets. Three-quarters of Northern Rock deposits were secured wholesale, primarily on very short-term conditions.

As already noted, transformation (borrowing short and lending long) is a traditional feature of banking activity. More and more institutions, however, took a gamble on the yield curve,

---

[27] A case in point is that of SIVs, which were financed almost entirely with short-term liabilities and in early August 2007 saw their financing costs explode as the interest rate on asset-backed commercial paper (i.e., liabilities between one day and six months collateralized by assets) moved from 5–10 basis points above the American overnight borrowing rate to 100 basis points (Tett 2009, 182).

[28] Deposit insurance in the United Kingdom was at the time poorly structured. Only £2,000 per person was completely covered by this insurance, the next £33,000 being guaranteed up to 90 percent. This partial insurance provided an incentive to run, even for depositors with very little savings in the bank. By comparison, deposit insurance in the United States was temporarily raised from the standard $100,000 to $250,000 until December 2009; deposits are fully insured up to €70,000 in France.

betting on short-term rates remaining low and access to whole-sale markets remaining easy. Several observations support this view.[29]

- Commercial banks pledged substantial liquidity support to the conduits, promising to supply liquidity in case the conduits had trouble finding funds in the wholesale market. According to Acharya and Schnabl (2009), the ten largest conduit administrators (mainly commercial banks) had a ratio of asset-backed commercial paper to equity ranging from 32.1 percent to 336.6 percent in January 2007. See the accompanying table, drawn from Acharya and Schnabl's chapter. These liquidity support pledges represented an elementary form of regulatory evasion. Such off-balance-sheet commitments carried much lower capital requirements than would have been the case had the liabilities been on the balance sheets.
- The increase in the market share of investment banks mechanically increased the financial sector's interest-rate fragility, as investment banks rely on repo and commercial-paper funding much more than commercial banks do.
- Primary dealers increased their overnight to term borrowing ratio.
- Leveraged buyouts have become more leveraged.
- Investment banks explained to their clients how to make high returns through derivative products that bet on falling interest rates.[30]

Five large investment banks,[31] lacking liquidity, either went bankrupt or merged with commercial banks, with the support of the U.S. government. Lehman Brothers was the biggest default in the history of the United States ($613 billion of debt, $639 billion of assets). In September 2008, Morgan Stanley and Goldman Sachs

---

[29] For more details on increased transformation, see Adrian and Shin (2008).

[30] See Tett (2009, 36).

[31] A merchant bank (also called an investment bank) has two main activities: (1) portfolio management (shares, debentures, etc.), and (2) market making and acting as a counterparty in over-the-counter (OTC) trading. Unlike commercial (retail) banks, investment banks do not take retail deposits and therefore are not subject to standard banking regulation.

Ten Largest Conduit Administrators by Size

	Conduits		Administrator			
	Number	CP (in £bn)	Assets (in £bn)	Equity (in £bn)	CP/Asset (%)	CP/Equity (%)
Citibank	23	93	1,884	120	4.9	77.4
ABN Amro	9	69	13,000	34	5.3	201.1
Bank of America	12	46	1,464	136	3.1	33.7
HBOS	2	44	1,160	42	3.8	105.6
JPMorgan Chase	9	42	1,352	116	3.1	36.1
HSBC	6	39	1,861	123	2.1	32.1
Société Générale	7	39	1,260	44	3.1	87.2
Deutsche Bank	14	38	1,483	44	2.6	87.8
Barclays	3	33	1,957	54	1.7	61.5
WestLB	8	30	376	9	8.0	336.6

Source: Acharya and Schnabl (2009)
CP = commercial paper

became bank holding companies. Merrill Lynch was bought by Bank of America, and Bear Stearns by JPMorgan Chase. Accordingly, all are now regulated by the Fed. Before then, the solvency and liquidity of investment banks had been subject to supervision by the Securities and Exchange Commission (SEC) since 2004, on a voluntary basis. The SEC had assigned the task of supervising investment banks (with $4,000 billion in assets) to just seven employees! Furthermore, the concern shown by these supervisors had been simply ignored.[32]

Thanks to the stability of their insured retail deposits, American commercial banks were initially slightly better able to withstand the crisis, even though various bankruptcies and the fragility of giants such as Citi and Bank of America remind us that retail banks also took gigantic risks and were highly dependant on wholesale short-term funding.[33]

. . . THAT PUTS MONETARY AUTHORITIES IN A BIND

The generalization of risk taking through high levels of transformation puts monetary authorities in a difficult position. Either they do not react when interest rates rise again (risking the bottom falling out of the financial system), or they yield and maintain interest rates at an artificially low level and indirectly bail out institutions that have taken excessive risks. Monetary authorities found themselves trapped by generalized transformation and, sure enough, the Fed funds rate fell from 5.25 percent on September 18, 2007, to 0 percent on December 16, 2008.

Farhi and Tirole (2009) show that keeping interest rates low has several costs beyond validating past excessive transformation:

First, as we have seen, loose monetary policy encourages institutions to persist with the same bad behavior, paving the way for the next crisis, through two channels: low short-term rates (1) make a short liability maturity structure appealing to financial institutions, and (2) boost financial institutions' leverage by lowering their overall cost of capital.

---

[32] See Labaton (2008).

[33] For a comparison of capital positions of retail and investment banks at the onset of the crisis, see Blundell-Wignall and Atkinson (2008).

Second, loose monetary policy distorts interest rates away from their natural level, discouraging savings; loose monetary policy may also distort relative prices and create inflation.

Third, a loose monetary policy transfers resources from lenders to borrowers; in particular, the recent episode has seen a sizable transfer from consumers to institutions through this channel, which is much less visible than ordinary (fiscal) bailouts.

To be clear—the central banks could not let institutions with excessive transformation go under by raising interest rates. They were "stuck." My point is that during the boom they should have prevented the emergence of this "fait accompli." Preventive measures were called for, as ex post toughness is neither desirable (despite the costs of leniency) nor credible. The solution in my view lies with monitoring transformation not only at the institution's level, but also overall. It is important that multiple "strategic" financial institutions do not simultaneously encounter refinancing problems, as was the case in the crisis.

Let us conclude this section with two remarks about maturity transformation and the sensitivity of balance sheets to interest-rate movements. First, maturity transformation is a natural way for financial institutions to correlate their risks (in this instance by betting on low interest rates), but it is by no means the only way. For example, before the crisis many financial institutions were simultaneously trying to increase their exposure to the subprime market to boost their returns.[34] While that market is itself influenced by the interest rate, it has other drivers, and so was another source of correlated distress.

Second, many observers[35] extol the merits of a "market solution" to the problem of insuring deposits in the banking sector. The idea is that the fees paid by the banks for deposit insurance

[34] E.g., Tett (2009, 124). Tett (p. 102) points at another, unexpected source of correlation: the use of the same statistical techniques (Li's Gaussian copula approach), the miscalibration of which introduced correlated errors. The common assumption that housing markets would remain relatively uncorrelated in the United States is a well-known mistake inducing correlation of positions.

[35] Basing their analysis on the pioneering work of Calomiris and Kahn (1991) and Diamond and Rajan (2001).

do not reflect the actual situation faced by the bank, and hence the anticipated cost of the guarantee. One should rather, the argument goes, index depositor insurance on the rates prevailing in the market for wholesale deposits, provided they were given a priority and a maturity date equivalent to that of retail deposits. The idea is seductive: the bank's borrowing rates on the wholesale market reflect the concern of sophisticated agents regarding the risk incurred by the creditors of the bank, including by small depositors. That Northern Rock and many other financial institutions were no longer able to refinance in the wholesale market under appropriate conditions demonstrates the limits of this strategy, however. First, significant resort to the wholesale market[36] increases transformation and exposes the bank to an increase in interest rates or a freeze in the interbank market. Second, indexing depositor insurance to the rates prevailing in the wholesale market exacerbates the funding difficulties when conditions deteriorate: a rise in insurance premiums when the bank becomes less solvent amplifies its losses and leads into a vicious circle.[37] Market solutions to the pricing of deposit insurance increase the sensitivity of balance sheets to the institution's ability to raise funds in the wholesale market.

Poor Risk Appraisal and the Evasion of Regulatory Capital Adequacy Requirements

Regulated financial institutions (commercial banks, insurance companies, pension funds, broker-dealers) are subject to requirements regarding the minimum level of their capital or equity. With regard to commercial banks, while the exact nature of regulation depends on the country and epoch (the account that follows is therefore of necessity broad-brush, and so I will stress the

---

[36] The importance of such resort underlies the integrity of the measurement of risk on the part of noninsured creditors. Were uninsured depositors required to take on only a small fraction of the risk, sweet deals would emerge allowing the bank to pay low rates on deposit insurance.

[37] See Dewatripont and Tirole (1994). For this reason some partisans of the market approach suggest using the information revealed by wholesale interest rates a bank has to pay purely as a signal that regulators should intervene and require the bank to downsize.

philosophy of regulation rather than its details), the Basel accords set a number of general principles. The idea is to maintain a cushion, the bank's capital, meant to allow it to absorb losses with a high probability, and so to protect depositors or the depositors' insurer, the deposit insurance fund. The Basel I accords (1988) defined two components of capital:

"Level 1" capital, the most important, including the issue of equity and retained earnings.

"Level 2" capital, comprising long-term (more than five-year) debt, hybrid capital—for example, preferred stock,[38] and some reserves.[39]

In a way, this hierarchy (and the exclusion of short-term debt) reflects the permanence of the bank's liabilities or, put differently, the pressure to disgorge cash. Although the accords focus on solvency, liquidity concerns are implicit in the definition of capital requirements, albeit in a very rough way. The ideal liability in this pecking order is equity, which is permanent and does not command an automatic dividend, followed by preferred stocks (which really are debt instruments, whose coupons can be deferred), and long-term debt.

Supervisors in charge of financial regulation have a complex task. First, balance sheets of financial institutions change rapidly, certainly much faster than that of industrial companies with limited involvement in financial markets. Second, financial techniques and instruments are subject to much innovation, some of which is designed to keep regulators in the dark. Third, regulators have limited means for oversight at their disposal and they compete for talented staff with much wealthier regulated institutions, funds,

[38] Preferred shares combine properties of both stocks and bonds. Like bonds, they specify a fixed payment and do give control to the borrower in normal times. Like shares, they involve flexibility in the terms of payment, and thus exert less pressure on the liquidity of the borrower than ordinary debt; the borrower can in effect delay payment (the borrower is unable to pay dividends on ordinary shares if payment on preferred shares is delayed—the priority of the latter is in effect with respect to ordinary shares).

[39] The minimum capital is 4 percent of assets (weighted by risk) for level 1, and a total of 8 percent for level 1 plus level 2 (the level 2 capital cannot exceed the level 1 capital for the purposes of calculating statutory capital). National regulators can demand higher ratios.

or rating agencies. Fourth, their independence is only partial: for instance, the favorable treatment of mortgage risk was a response to demands made by American politicians.

Fifth, competition with other regulators, or with an absence of regulation, also complicates the regulators' job. Regulated institutions compete with unregulated ones in some market segments. For example, in the 1990s commercial banks successfully lobbied regulators to undervalue risk on their trading book, on the (correct) grounds that they were subject to competition in trading activities from unregulated institutions. This lobbying resulted in exceedingly low capital requirements on trading risk. Accordingly, capital requirements for the trading book are currently being revised upward.

Regulated institutions also take advantage of competition among regulators to be the "most accommodating."[40] Regulatory competition has always existed at the international level, because institutions can choose in which country their head office is registered. But there is also competition among regulators in the same country. In the United States, Countrywide Financial changed its regulator in the spring of 2007 to escape regulation it considered too constraining. The institution was welcomed with open arms by the Office of Thrift Supervision (OTS), whose budget depended on payments made by the institutions it regulated. The OTS traditionally regulated savings banks and real estate lenders. Those banks heavily involved in housing loans could therefore choose to be regulated by the OTS, which was well known for its lenient approach to the supervision of mortgage risk. Countrywide Financial soon got into difficulties and, on the brink of collapse, was bought by the Bank of America, while three other large banks supervised by the OTS (Washington Mutual, IndyMac Bankcorp, and Downey S&L Association) were taken under the wing of the U.S. government.[41]

---

[40] It is not always in a bank's interest to be regulated too lightly, however, since this might cause it to lose credibility. The bank therefore has to reach a compromise between leveraging its equity (as tolerated by its supervisor) and its credibility in the marketplace. Empirically, though, the demand for "light-touch" regulation often seems to win out.

[41] For more details, see Appelbaum and Nakashima (2008a).

Financial institutions have exploited imperfections in regulatory measurement of risk to underestimate[42] their capital requirements, hence increasing their return on equity. For example,

1. As we have seen, banks pledged off-balance-sheet liquidity support to conduits, which involved very low capital requirements (10 percent of what would have been required, had the assets remained on the balance sheet). Citibank, Bank of America, and other banks all issued liquidity options that were a variant of lines of credit transferred off the balance sheet, allowing CDOs to use "liquidity puts" to make up for the shortfall in liquidity if they (generally financed by short-term debt) were no longer able to place their commercial paper. For instance, Citibank ended up with an exposure (to which it gave little publicity) of $25 billion to CDOs that it had initiated.[43]

2. Banks covered some of their risk by buying insurance from credit enhancers (the monolines) that were themselves undercapitalized.

3. Banks rescued conduits they had no duty to rescue. Bear Stearns, for example, went far beyond its legal obligations by bailing out some funds it had no obligation to rescue. It is clear that Bear Stearns was not tightly regulated; but more generally, banks could be led to bail out financial instruments they had created, even if they were not obliged to do so and without any capital contribution for the corresponding "reputation risk."

4. The transition to new procedural rules (Basel II) had been anticipated since 2004. An important aspect of the revision

[42] A case in point is Lehman Brothers, which a few days before bankruptcy boasted a Tier 1 capital ratio of 11 percent (recall that the regulatory requirement is 4 percent).

[43] The conduits involved super-senior notes (the more senior part of the capital structure), which were supposed to be completely safe and were routinely assigned AAA ratings. Unlike unregulated investment banks, such as Bear Stearns, Lehman Brothers, and Morgan Stanley, which had substantial super-senior exposures on their balance sheets, Citi, a retail bank, was constrained by leverage ceilings and therefore moved the risk off its balance sheet. See Tett (2009, 135–136, 205).

to the regulatory framework is that the weight allocated to mortgage lending was reduced from 50 percent to 35 percent. That meant that the capital requirement of banks was reduced by 30 percent in this sector of activity. This probably reinforced the already strong interest in anything related to housing mortgages.

5. Finally, for all the previously stated caveats about the difficulty of their job, regulators showed themselves to be slack. They not only lacked information about the risks attached to the new products but also let themselves be lobbied by the industry; see, for example, the aptly titled chapter "Dancing around Regulators" in Tett (2009) for a history of the debate on the regulation of derivatives. For more on this topic, see chapter 3 in this volume.

The Procyclical Nature of Regulation

Capital requirements are in principle invariant through the cycle. For a commercial bank, one dollar of capital has to be set off against 12.5 dollars of assets weighted according to risk, no matter what the state of the economy might be. Yet, financial intermediaries are induced to build up their assets rapidly in good periods and to reduce them in periods of recession. Mark-to-market accounting—or more generally fair value accounting—mandates that financial intermediaries recognize the appreciation or depreciation of their assets when the market value is directly available, or reconstitute prices through related assets' market prices, when available.[44]

Faced with a decrease in the price of their assets in a downturn, financial intermediaries must respond to a shortage of capital by

reestablishing their equity by issuing new equity to individuals or institutions with some financial "muscle";[45]

---

[44] They must also in principle reflect the deterioration in the solvency of the counterparties, itself very closely related to the economic cycle.

[45] Examples ranged from Warren Buffet to sovereign funds, Bank of America (which is now in financial straits, but at the time acquired Countrywide Financial, the largest mortgage lender in the United States, and Merrill Lynch), BNP-

or reducing the size of their balance sheet by reselling assets; or reducing the size of their balance sheet by stopping lending.

The first of these alternatives has been heavily used. But this solution has its limits. First, investors with financial muscle may prefer to wait until share prices fall even further to make acquisitions. Also, investors could well be reluctant to buy shares in a business that may have many skeletons in its closet. In addition, deep pockets are limited during difficult periods. Finally, some investors, such as sovereign funds, who had stepped in to rescue distressed institutions, had been burned by losses and became reluctant to commit further funds. Overall, in September 2008, only 72 percent of American banks' losses had been made good by injections of new capital.

The second alternative involves offloading assets. Assets may have to be sold at fire-sale prices, however, when many institutions subject to capital requirements sell off assets at the same time. Some, like Ben Bernanke and Hank Paulson when preparing the Paulson Plan in September 2008, even argued that assets were selling below their fundamental value, suggesting that some asset markets were characterized by a "negative bubble."

Private and Public Liquidity

INADEQUATE AND POORLY REDISPATCHED
PRIVATE-SECTOR LIQUIDITY

Industrial companies and financial institutions both rely on access to cash to finance investment or current expenditures. For this purpose, they need liquid assets—that is, assets that can be quickly sold without incurring major losses. Across the economy as a whole, "private-sector liquidity" or "inside liquidity" comes from previously issued securities (bonds, shares, etc.) that can be quickly sold by their holders as needed at low transaction cost.

How much liquidity is effectively available also depends on whether it is efficiently redispatched. The future is uncertain for both business enterprises and financial institutions, and not only at the macroeconomic level: some economic agents will turn out

---

Paribas, BBVA, HSBC, and Santander in Europe, and Japanese firms that made foreign acquisitions worth $71 billion between January and November 2008.

to have important cash requirements while others will have a surplus of cash. Liquidity must therefore be well reallocated. This process of reallocation in practice takes place in a number of ways:

> ex post, in an unprogrammed way through borrowings in the money market and securitization or sale of assets;
>
> or, alternatively, ex ante, through advance agreements specifying reallocations of liquidity, such as a line of credit granted to an enterprise by a financial intermediary (guaranteeing the enterprise an option of access to new borrowing), or with an insurance contract, such as a credit-default swap (CDS).[46]

The crisis exhibited not only an overall shortage of liquidity but also a limited reallocation of liquidity from cash-rich to cash-poor institutions.

First, the liquidity of mortgage-backed securities shrank markedly when the risk of default was recognized. It is important to note that it is not bad news itself that creates a lack of liquidity but rather the amplification of the informational asymmetries created by bad news (otherwise, prices will simply fall without having an impact on the liquidity of securities). As has been outlined very clearly by Bengt Holmström (2008), safe assets are very liquid because potential buyers know their value. As soon as bad news casts doubt on the real value of an asset, potential purchasers begin to ask questions and adverse selection (worries that the other side to the transaction could be more knowledgeable than oneself about the true value of the asset) begins to freeze up markets.[47] Put differently, owners of such assets are exposed to a "double whammy": not only does the asset price fall but also the market is marred by adverse selection and becomes illiquid (selling the asset may involve substantial discounts relative to even the reduced value that the seller attached to the asset).

Second, doubt about the value of assets transforms into doubt about the soundness of the institutions holding them. In the recent crisis, those economic agents that had excess liquidity be-

---

[46] A CDS is a financial instrument insuring the buyer against default on a given piece of debt. The buyer pays a stream of fees in exchange for the insurance.

[47] The market becomes a "market for lemons." Since Akerlof's pioneering work in 1970 such markets have been extensively studied.

come reluctant to lend it to those that needed cash. In particular, the interbank market froze up.[48] The loss of confidence in the accuracy of ratings of securitized portfolios; the questioning of the liquidity of (former) investment banks, hedge funds, bond insurers, insurance companies, leveraged buyouts, and even commercial banks; and more generally a significant lack of information on the size of the losses taken by counterparties, directly or indirectly—all of this meant that no one had any confidence in anyone else anymore.

Take the example of the credit derivatives market. It notionally totaled $62,000 billion in September 2008, when the financial markets became most concerned about systemic risk. This number is of course highly misleading, as it represents the gross value of securities against which contracts had been written. Much of this can be netted across banks. But the uncertainty about the net amounts and their structure (the matrix of cross-exposures) suffices to scare the markets. As Caballero and Simsek (2009) emphasize, the task of knowing not only whether one's counterparties are solvent but also whether one's counterparties' counterparties are, their counterparties are, and so on, becomes daunting in times of generalized distress.

A case in point is AIG. At the point when it was salvaged by the U.S. government,[49] the insurer AIG had sold banks and other investors $441 billion of protection on fixed-income securities through credit-default swaps, creating considerable risks for banks linked to AIG.[50] AIG had promised to post collateral to

[48] An indication of this situation is given by the TED spread, the difference between the three-month LIBOR rate (the London Interbank Offered Rate for noncollateralized interbank borrowing) and the rate of treasury bills over the same term. On October 15, 2008, this difference was 4.2 percent, compared to 0.2 percent at the beginning of 2007.

[49] AIG was rescued two days after Lehman was allowed to go under. The Fed's immediate action was to lend $85 billion in exchange for a 79.9 percent stake in AIG (i.e., nationalizing it).

[50] AIG had a core business of traditional insurance that was quite healthy; but this core activity was progressively overshadowed by the institution's activities in derivatives markets. AIG was judged "too risky to fail," or rather "too interconnected to fail," and, as discussed in the previous footnote, on September 16, 2008, it received emergency support from the Fed—a line of credit with a two-year maturity period—of $85 billion. By November 10, 2008, the total amount of support advanced by the Fed and the U.S. Treasury was $150 billion.

back up the contingent liability it acquired by insuring super-senior CDO debt; but by and large AIG failed to abide by its obligation.[51] One can only imagine what would have happened if a few days after the Lehman episode AIG had defaulted.

When doubts arise about the solvency of some player in an opaque network of mutual exposures, even borrowers who are by themselves quite sound become suspect. Such distrust, or adverse selection, is an amplification factor: markets lock up and agents possessing funds for investment place them only short term and only with extremely safe borrowers (the so-called flight to quality). The obvious recipient of funds in a flight to quality is the U.S. government. Indeed, just after the Lehman and AIG events, sovereign wealth funds, which had previously invested in the shares of Western banks and lost a great deal of money, placed a good part of their $2–3 trillion in U.S. Treasury bonds.[52] Similarly, private equity firms were sitting on $450 billion available for investment. Overall, Treasury bonds and central bank deposits became extremely attractive. This hoarding was further encouraged by the central banks' policy of paying interest on deposits.[53]

In sum, the freezing up of interbank markets hampers the reallocation of liquidity and amplifies the problems arising from a shortage of aggregate liquidity.

PUBLIC PROVISION OF LIQUIDITY

Economic theory stresses the necessity for the state to boost industrial and financial sectors during periods of liquidity shortage.[54] "Outside liquidity" is created through the government's injection of funds into the economy, especially in times of recession. This involves bailing out economic agents, using forbearance in the implementation of capital requirements, following

---

[51] Tett (2009, 237).

[52] Sovereign funds underwrote some 60 percent of recapitalizations in the second half of 2007 and only 7 percent during the first half of 2008 (International Monetary Fund 2008).

[53] For example, on September 28, 2008, banks had €102.8 billion deposited with the ECB.

[54] This is an old theme, dating back at least to Keynes and Hicks. For microfoundations, see, e.g., Holmström and Tirole (1998).

countercyclical monetary policy, providing deposit insurance and unemployment payments not indexed over the cycle, implementing countercyclical fiscal policy, and so on. Outside liquidity comes from the government's unique ability to pledge current and future generations of households' money through regalian taxation power. All of these practices share an explicit or implicit transfer of resources from households to industrial and (more often) financial sectors in periods of recession. But they also share the unintended consequence of bailing out those who have taken big risks.[55]

Since August 2007, European and American central banks have repeatedly injected liquidity into their economies. They have relaxed their collateral quality requirements (accepting even subprime paper) and have extended the range of actors they could lend to and the maturity of lending.[56] Nominal interest rates have converged on zero. The U.S. real estate market received support through the extension of loan limits by the Federal Housing Administration and the extension of mortgage ceilings by Fannie Mae and Freddie Mac. They have rescued or helped both financial institutions and industrial companies.[57] With all the caveats given earlier and additional ones relative to moral hazard, the injection of liquidity appears to have been opportune.

---

[55] This view is held by, among others, Shiller (2009, chapter 5).

[56] For example, in the United States through the Term Auction Facility (depository institutions), the Primary Dealer Credit Facility, and a host of other facilities (the Asset-Backed Commercial Paper Money Market Mutual Fund (ABCP MMMF) Liquidity Facility, the Commercial Paper Funding Facility, the Money Market Investor Funding Facility, and the Term Asset-Backed Securities Loan Facility).

[57] One remarkable development was the proposal made by the U.S. Treasury at the beginning of October 2008 to authorize the Fed to repurchase short-term noncollateralized debt issued by firms, an action that is neither part of the responsibilities nor a domain of expertise of a central bank. The prospect of direct subsidies to firms reflected growing alarm about the contraction of credit to firms, which has been more severe than that traditionally observed when the capitalization of the banking system is degraded. Meanwhile, the freeze in the bond market (which primarily affects large enterprises, which have by far the best access to that market) implied that even the best firms had difficulty refinancing. Although it is easy to understand this reaction, to see the Fed become the "buyer of last resort" and bypass the intermediaries is disquieting.

PRINCIPLES FOR BAILOUTS

The bailout of banks in most countries in the world raises questions as to how the state should proceed. Every choice of bailout policy involves trade-offs.

There are simple rules governing the recapitalization of an institution by the state: first, the state has to be compensated whenever feasible. Second, the institution has to be placed under greater supervision. Finally, when the institution is verging on failure, shareholders should receive nothing. There are three reasons for this last rule: first, the value of shares in the alternative (i.e., collapse) is equal to zero; nothing should be given to managers and shareholders who had brought about losses for creditors as well as third parties (employees, the state). Second, public finances, already stretched in ordinary times, are particularly so during crises. Gifts to shareholders amount to a useless waste of ammunition.[58] Finally, this approach gives directors an incentive to come forward and negotiate with the government before it is too late.

Another issue concerns the form of state participation. Several nonexclusive alternatives can be envisaged:

Temporary nationalization. This approach was adopted by the Scandinavian countries when their entire banking system was on the verge of collapse in the early 1990s. The Scandi-

---

[58] The treatment of creditors is much more difficult. The expropriation of short-term creditors speeds up the expectation of a lack of liquidity on the part of institutions in difficulty. Without wishing to automatically guarantee all deposits (which is what a number of European countries did in October 2008), one must acknowledge that unfavorable treatment of these creditors will only exacerbate the crisis. But the sole expropriation of long-term creditors is far from ideal, either, because if expected, it forces banks to have very short-term liabilities, creating liquidity problems. Finally, it is clear that extending guarantees to wholesale debt instruments creates moral hazard, as creditors, short- or long-term, no longer pay attention to the solvency of the institution; it might therefore only hold if supervisory scrutiny is rigorous and capital requirements strictly enforced, making the absence of market monitoring less costly (although some would argue that market monitoring and regulation are complementary). On the relationship between regulation and financial market monitoring, see, e.g., Faure-Grimaud's (2002) analysis of the regulation of network industries.

navian approach was to take the banks under the wing of the state, recapitalize them,[59] attempt to run them on essentially commercial lines so as to minimize the final cost to the taxpayer, and then resell their assets as soon as possible in the form of an initial public offering or a negotiated sale. This approach allows the state to supervise and control risk, but creates a managerial problem, as government representatives usually do not have the knowledge or the proper incentives to run the business (they also have to be able to resist political pressure seeking to make use of a nationalized bank for industrial policy, pork barrel, and so forth).

Participation by taking up preferred (nonvoting) stocks and warrants.[60] This approach[61] has the benefit of leaving management in private hands, which presumably are more familiar with techniques and risks and less susceptible to political pressure. By contrast, there is a real danger that private shareholders might gamble if the capitalization is inadequate, since this strategy allows them to benefit from the "upside." The existence of an option (defined by the warrants) to convert preferred stocks into shares reduces incentives for shareholders to take such risks, since if the institution becomes profitable again, they will be able to share in the gains by exercising their options. But it does not entirely eliminate shareholders' incentives to gamble for resurrection.

Separating toxic assets ("bad bank") from healthy assets ("good bank"), and the retention of the latter within the institution and transfer of the former to a defeasance structure. This approach is a variant of the option of temporary nationalization, which shares the defects of this option: weak incentives for those administering the defeasance structure (and

[59] At no small cost. The recapitalization of Nordbanken in Sweden, for example, cost about 3 percent of GDP.

[60] This was, for example, what Warren Buffet did in restoring Goldman Sachs to solvency.

[61] There are many variants of this approach. For example, in the proposed sale of Wachovia to Citigroup in September 2008, the latter agreed to absorb up to $42 billion of losses on $312 billion of loans, the FDIC taking on the residual risk in exchange for warrants and preferred shares. In October 2008, however, Wachovia was taken over by Wells Fargo without FDIC involvement.

their personal interest in shifting all responsibility to previous management teams), and transfer at low prices to other financial intermediaries.[62] But it does allow the balance sheet to be cleaned up and it eliminates incentives to gamble for resurrection.[63]

The optimal—or, I should say, least bad—approach depends on circumstances. If a bank defaults on payments and has to be rescued overnight, the simplest solution is for the government to buy shares in the bank, amounting to temporary nationalization. The bank's directors are replaced and the value of the shares completely wiped out. As we have seen, this has many advantages, including giving both directors and shareholders an incentive to approach the government about to their difficulties before it becomes too late.

To get banks to come to authorities—and for the latter to intervene—before things get really bad, the government can, for example, take up preferred shares and warrants.[64] Management teams can then be retained if their performance is decent, avoiding the appointment of new managers lacking in experience and knowledge of the financial institution. Making resort to the state an attractive option for banks that are in difficulty, however, confronts the stigma problem. Because institutions also rely on markets for their funding, they are usually very reluctant to be involved with the state in a visible way, thereby signaling fragility. Stigmatization is a familiar phenomenon, as it also makes banks reluctant to use the discount window, emerging countries to seek

---

[62] Because the corresponding assets are mostly illiquid, it is difficult in retrospect to prove that such a transfer involved negligence, or corruption in extreme cases.

[63] A variant of this course of action is the provision of a guarantee for a limited assortment of toxic assets. For example, the purchase by J. P. Morgan of Bear Stearns for more or less nothing when it was close to failure in March 2008 was made on condition that a $30 billion line of credit be granted by the New York Fed. J. P. Morgan assumed responsibility for the first $1 billion of Bear Stearns losses, the Fed taking on $29 billion of doubtful debt.

[64] Recapitalization will of course be required by the banking regulator. We should also note that financial institutions would wish to maintain their independence and would have a tendency to resist actions taken by the government. They will therefore advocate equity participation by the government without right of control, such as mezzanine debt or nonvoting preferred shares.

lines of credit from the International Monetary Fund (the IMF's contingent credit lines, introduced in 1999, were never used; the facility was allowed to expire in 2003 on its scheduled sunset date), and financial institutions eager to quickly reimburse their Troubled Asset Relief Program (TARP) loans.[65]

The Japanese experience demonstrates the extent of the stigma problem. In November 1997, unable to suppress the crisis by purchasing toxic securities, the Japanese government made available up to $124 billion in mezzanine debt to undercapitalized banks. Those who took advantage of this, ultimately under government pressure, were among the healthiest, and they borrowed only $17 billion. The state offered an additional $71 billion in 1999, this time in a mixture of mezzanine debt and preferred shares, with the option to convert these into ordinary shares.[66]

LOAN GUARANTEES IN INTERBANK OR MONETARY MARKETS

The guarantee of interbank borrowing eliminates distrust in lending between banks and so stimulates the market. The policy of guaranteeing interbank lending does have its limits, however.

First, it provides no reassurance to markets concerning the solvency of borrowing institutions. As a consequence, this insurance has to be extended to other providers of liquidity to banks in the money market if it is to have a significant impact.

This leads into the second point, involving the purpose of such a measure: an interbank loan underwritten by state guarantee is in effect a loan from the state to the borrowing bank (whether fees are levied on this state guarantee or not). All the benefit of interbank borrowing (the mutual scrutiny of banking institutions) vanishes. For example, the interbank market would be able to lend large sums to a distressed bank at a rate equal to the market rate if the banking supervisor were not to act quickly and prevent it.

Of course, the state can levy an actuarially fair insurance premium, and does so in practice. Such premiums accentuate the

---

[65] Of course, this is not the only reason for the recent rush to reimburse TARP support, as the support is linked to increased supervision and public attention, as well as extra constraints (including on compensation).

[66] For an account of stigma and bailout policies in Japan, see Hoshi and Kashyap (2008).

phenomenon of adverse selection, however: only banks in genuine difficulty will be prepared to borrow at the corresponding interest rate (premium included), increasing risks and thus the actuarial premium that banks have to pay for insurance, and so forth. This well-known phenomenon is the reason that, more generally, credit markets clear through rationing, and not through the interest rate.

The Fuzzy Frontier between Regulated and Unregulated Spheres, Plus a Lethal Mix of Public and Private

TAXPAYER INVOLVEMENT WITHOUT ADEQUATE SUPERVISION AND PROTECTION

The classic form of intervention in a financial crisis involves the bailout of retail banking establishments or other institutions within the regulated sphere (insurance companies, pension funds). The large mutual exposures between the regulated sector and very lightly regulated or unregulated institutions (investment banks, hedge funds, private equity, and so on) have completely blurred the picture in this respect. In the recent crisis, authorities rescued or contemplated rescuing entities that lay outside the regulated sphere by injecting capital, by repurchasing shares, or, more simply, by keeping interest rates low. In a nutshell, institutions from the unregulated sphere had access to taxpayers' money without having to subject themselves to prudential regulation and without having to contribute to deposit insurance funds. They had their cake and ate it too.

This fuzziness is illustrated by the debate over the refusal of American authorities to rescue Lehman Brothers. American taxpayers' money had earlier been used to save another large merchant bank, Bear Stearns. Letting Lehman go under had tremendous consequences for the financial markets and was generally considered a mistake. But it illustrates well the dilemma: looking at the situation (ex post), American authorities had little choice but to rescue large interconnected institutions—which they did, except in Lehman's case.

Interestingly, even in the Lehman case, many money market funds and other institutions had purchased debt issued by Lehman Brothers in the months before its collapse because they were convinced that the U.S. government would rescue Lehman; this demonstrates how widely involved taxpayer money was presumed to be by the market.

But viewed from an ex ante perspective, an ex post rescue seems completely unwarranted, and so steps should be taken to avoid being confronted with such unpalatable choices. It becomes urgent to take measures to prevent authorities in the future from being held hostage by the risk of an unregulated institution defaulting, because it cannot be right that firms subject to no external controls should enjoy access to taxpayer funding.

Leaving aside Freddie Mac and Fannie Mae, to which we will turn next, the main beneficiaries of direct or indirect bailouts outside the regulated sector have been the large investment banks and AIG's holding company (which was basically an investment bank). Because large investment banks have disappeared (Lehman, which was liquidated, and Bear Stearns, purchased by J. P. Morgan, a bank holding company) or became bank holding companies (Goldman Sachs, Morgan Stanley), the concern has since turned more toward hedge funds, which will be asked to be more transparent. After all, the Fed in 1998 already organized a rescue plan and reduced its interest rates several times in order to prevent the default of a speculative fund, Long Term Capital Management (LTCM). The leaders at the G20 London summit (April 2, 2009) opted to extend oversight to "all systemically important financial institutions, instruments and markets," including systemically important hedge funds.

Although there is nothing wrong with hedge fund transparency, such measures in my view are unlikely to be effective. First, regulatory agencies struggle to regulate existing institutions; enlarging the scope of regulation will require a very large increase in their resources. Second, the state is shooting at a moving target. Many unregulated firms can become hedge funds. It is not hard to imagine that the state might be tempted to bail out other types of institutions. There is no reason that interconnected non-banking firms would not gain access to the same recapitalization schemes and guarantee of medium-term debt as those financial institutions that have been bailed out.

FREDDIE MAC AND FANNIE MAE

On September 7, 2008, Henry Paulson, then the U.S. secretary of the treasury, announced the rescue of two government-sponsored enterprises (GSEs), Fannie Mae and Freddie Mac, whose main activity consisted of buying mortgages on the secondary market, pooling them, and selling them as mortgage-backed securities to investors on the open market. Their activities were restricted to so-called conforming loans that satisfy certain criteria, in particular debt-to-income ratio limits and documentation requirements. The two private institutions insured or guaranteed 40 to 50 percent (and in 2007 up to about 80 percent) of outstanding mortgage loans in the United States.[67] The rescue plan placed them under conservatorship and put together a refinancing package.

These two institutions are something of an anomaly. As private-sector bodies, their profits did not flow into the public purse. But they did enjoy a guarantee from the U.S. government. The general perception was that, if they got into difficulties, they would be bailed out by the federal government—which was, in effect, what happened. As in the hallowed formula, the profits were privatized and the losses nationalized. And these GSEs were not subject to very rigorous regulation.[68] The European Commission has, by contrast, used European laws on state aid to prevent European governments[69] from extending implicit state guarantees and to limit a concoction of measures such as that which now threatens to be an additional heavy burden of public debt in the United States.

---

[67] According to the IMF's *Global Stability Report* (International Monetary Fund 2008, chapter 1), the losses of these two institutions amounted to $100–135 billion. Estimates later in 2008 put the total figure at $200 billion.

[68] Their regulator was the Department of Housing and Urban Development, which lacks expertise in systemic regulation and has an agenda relative to the housing market.

[69] As with Crédit Foncier, for example.

Inadequate Internal Controls and Compensation

RISK CONTROL

The balance sheet of a financial institution is peculiar. First, it can be altered very rapidly. In comparison, a manufacturer's assets (e.g., the tools of the trade of an electrician or automaker) change slowly.[70] Second, without very strict internal controls, it can be affected negatively and substantially by employees who do not belong to the team of managers. Individual traders can build up extremely dangerous positions (for example, Barings Bank and Société Générale). Managers and boards of directors have a great deal of trouble identifying the risks to which their institution is exposed.[71] Internal controls are therefore indispensable. Yet managers and prudential supervisors have long realized the complexity and difficulties of internal control. Internal risk managers were not very effective in preventing widespread gambling in the years preceding the recent crisis.

Even if risk managers are knowledgeable in their area of oversight, they tend to be somewhat cut off from trading floors, to forestall any suggestion of collusion. Therefore risk managers are exposed to informational asymmetries with respect to those who seek to involve the institution in deals; the informational asymmetries are all the greater if they have a reputation for rigor, as supervisees are then particularly unwilling to communicate information.[72]

Furthermore, compensation packages of risk managers must not create conflicts of interest, as when, for example, their bonuses are connected to the institution's business activity. Thus, the Financial Stability Forum (2009) argues that the staff engaged in risk control should not have their compensation linked to that of frontline business areas.

---

[70] Important decisions, such as mergers and acquisitions, are in principle examined carefully by the board of directors. Of course, I realize that large manufacturers (say, Airbus or General Electric) are also involved in financial operations. The point made here is that the balance sheets of financial institutions may change particularly quickly.

[71] On this last point, the recent case of Citigroup (which in 2007 had 375,000 employees) is instructive. See the interesting piece by Dash and Creswell (2008).

[72] These problems are very well treated in Anon (2008).

Also, playing the role of the killjoy, risk managers often are in a position of opposing the taking of profitable positions so as to occasionally avoid very large losses. That is, most of the time they will tend to reduce short-run profitability. It is therefore not surprising that, although the power of risk managers becomes important in time of crisis, it remains weak during normal periods, which leads to important risks being taken. There is a strong temptation in expansionary periods to allow considerations of short-term profitability to sideline risk managers.

Correspondingly, and assuming that risk managers are incentivized to reduce risk, they are unlikely to succeed in doing so if the upper management's compensation and career concerns make it shortsighted. This brings us to the topical issue of managerial compensation.

MANAGERIAL COMPENSATION

Managerial compensation has been a clear and natural target of criticism. It is now widely acknowledged that bankers' pay packages induced a short-term focus, so management did not represent the best interests of shareholders. Furthermore, extremely high leverage strengthened the incentive of the owners of shares and options to gamble at creditors' expense.[73] Executive compensation has long been subject to economists' and policy makers' criticism; see, for example, Bebchuk and Fried (2004) for a scathing precrisis analysis. The debate on executive compensation is particularly important in the area of banking, as regulators are meant to protect both depositors and taxpayer money.

The very generous compensation of failed managers has been quite shocking, even from a strictly economic (incentives) perspective. The stock options and bonuses granted before the collapse rewarded underperformance, not excellence.

The sheer size and the structure of compensation packages in the financial sector pose problems. And the many scandals related to the swift exercise of stock options a few months before the accrual of bad news about the institution demonstrate that compensation committees have been far more complacent with managers than principles of good governance would suggest. But

---

[73] See Bebchuk and Spamann (forthcoming).

even if directors sitting on compensation committees are not too complacent, they are unlikely to represent the interests of the deposit insurance fund and the taxpayers, and therefore are likely to approve managerial incentive schemes that induce too much risk taking.

FURTHER DISCUSSION

Compensation is not the entire story. Long after the crisis had started, Dick Fuld, Lehman's CEO,[74] took enormous gambles on structured finance products at a time when no one else wanted to hold them anymore. Of course, this strategy would have made him fabulously rich had it succeeded. But the desire to be number one and the "Goldman syndrome" (trying to prove one can do as well as Goldman Sachs, the industry's benchmark) seem to have played a big role in his motivation.

PART II: HOW SHOULD THE FINANCIAL SYSTEM BE REFORMED?

To avoid a repetition of the financial crisis, we need both to change public policies that contributed to the crisis (particularly the mortgage crisis) and to institute financial reforms.

Desirable reforms of public policy regarding real estate lending include promoting consumer protection and reducing subsidies. First, to strengthen consumer protection, governments should at the very least make sure that all households, especially poor ones that do not have much access to financial information, are fully knowledgeable of the hazards associated with different kinds of loans.[75] Indeed, the U.S. Treasury's June 2009 proposal includes the creation of a consumer financial protection agency.[76] Second, the reduction or elimination of direct and indirect subsidies of

---

[74] Who had been chosen as the number one CEO by several specialized magazines in 2006!

[75] Shiller (2009, chapter 6) proposes that the U.S. government subsidize universal financial advice that is fee-only, comprehensive, and independent (i.e., offered by advisors not accepting remuneration from third parties).

[76] Clearly, such an agency must protect consumers from all unscrupulous lenders, not just in the traditional banking industry. Indeed, most of the risky subprime mortgages originated in the shadow (unregulated) banking system.

home ownership in the United States would seem to be appropriate. As Shiller (2009) notes, although it is true that home ownership creates a sense of personal investment in the community, the cost of recent policies promoting home ownership is incommensurate with the benefits.

Thoroughgoing reforms of the financial system are also necessary to prevent a repetition of the global crisis. Many of the mechanisms that currently prevail in financial markets have to be reviewed, either in principle or in application. Confronted with the financial tempest that had quickly engulfed the globe, the G20 member states came to an agreement at the Washington summit of November 15, 2008, on a process intended to promote better regulation of financial markets. They took first steps at the April 2, 2009, London meeting.[77] Meanwhile, regional initiatives are emerging in parallel.

I turn now to some of the financial reforms that in my view are key to avoiding a repeat of the recent episode.

Return to the Basics of Financial Regulation

WHAT IS PRUDENTIAL REGULATION ABOUT?

It is important to keep in mind what financial regulation is meant to achieve. The primary rationale for regulation is to protect small depositors, holders of insurance policies, or investors in pension funds, or the public insurer of the corresponding assets, from the default of those financial institutions. Where the government risks bailing out distressed financial intermediaries, then it becomes a matter of protecting taxpayers' money as well.

The second function of prudential regulation is to contain domino effects, that is, systemic risk. This motive may coincide with the first, as when supervisors want to avoid a domino effect in which the failure of a retail bank would have an impact on other retail banks. But as the recent crisis demonstrates, authorities may find themselves involved more generally in the maintenance of the financial system's integrity. And indeed, they have

---

[77] I will review some of these measures later. Others, such as the actions against tax havens and the strengthening of IMF responsibilities, are important but less central to the main theme of this chapter: prudential reforms.

rescued many large institutions (merchant banks, AIG's holding company) that have no small depositors.

The prevailing regulations for commercial banks derive from the Basel Accords of 1988 (Basel I), which require that the financial intermediary have sufficient capital (an equity buffer). The choice of a capital requirement involves a trade-off. On the one hand, banks have to be sufficiently capitalized so that savers or taxpayers do not suffer from possible losses. On the other, too strict a regulatory framework would prevent financial intermediaries from fulfilling their economic missions: the financing of investment in firms, especially small and medium enterprises, and the provision of liquidity to firms and markets.

Basel I requires the bank to make a capital provision (8 percent of risk-weighted assets) commensurate with the riskiness of loans, a safe loan (such as holding a Treasury bond) not requiring any capital provision. Regulators and financial institutions have long been aware of the mechanical nature of capital requirements. For example, the formula for capital requirements is purely additive; the total capital requirement is just the sum of the capital requirements for each loan, regardless of the correlation between the different risks (interest-rate risk, exchange-rate risk, credit risk, housing-market risk, etc.). Also, in Basel I all loans to corporations carry the same weight (an eight-cent capital requirement for a loan of one dollar), the holding of an AAA security requiring the same capital as that of a junk bond.

Rules were adjusted after 1988 to reflect such concerns. Basel II (2007), following similar rules for insurance companies, broker-dealers, and pension funds, allows for the use of the ratings produced by an agreed list of agencies to adjust capital requirements according to the quality of the assets. This new regulatory framework also authorizes large banks to use their own "internal models" to measure risks and hence the level of capital requirement, allowing supervisors to intervene with recapitalization requirements or to limit activities when signals turn ominous. Chapter 3 deals in depth with the issue of the measurement of risk in Basel II, and so I will devote only limited space to the matter.

The transition from Basel I to Basel II is illustrative of the classic dilemma involved in the choice between mechanical rules and the granting of a greater freedom to institutions. Basel I set up a

mechanical, non-market-oriented measurement of equity requirements. These requirements were quite removed from risk fundamentals, but they limited the scope for manipulation. Basel II
gives banks much more flexibility, allowing for better risk assessment where system and process have integrity; but the new rules
require more rigorous supervision and substantial trust in the
integrity of the various players. The bank's internal models, even
if endorsed by supervisors, create substantial freedom for less
scrupulous banks. Similarly, the extensive use of ratings makes
it necessary that rating agencies not enter into collusion with industry and that they exercise due diligence in rating firms.

The economic theory of collusion offers some commonsense
rules. Every increase in the flexibility of evaluation has to be
matched by a greater distance between evaluators (rating agencies, regulatory supervisors) and the evaluated (banks). Increased
flexibility magnifies the stakes for those who are supervised and
therefore increases lobbying and the danger of capture. Con-
versely, if one fears for the integrity of supervision and evaluation,
mechanical rules are called for. Some have, accordingly, suggested
that the use of ratings be abandoned for regulatory purposes. Although I do not support this position, I concur that rating agencies must demonstrate greater integrity in the way they arrive at
a credit rating if their ratings are to be used by supervisors.[78]

THE SCOPE OF REGULATION

There have been several calls for broadening the scope of financial regulation, covering more and more financial institutions.
The leaders at the G20 meeting in London moved in this direction. The June 2009 Obama administration plan would subject
to regulation all financial firms posing systemic risks, labeled
"tier 1" institutions. Such systemic risk regulation might be performed by the Fed, working with other regulators.[79]

[78] Or more generally by the public sphere. For example the Fed's TALF (Term
Asset-Backed Securities Loan Facility) accepts as collateral only securities that
have been rated by at least two NRSROs (nationally recognized statistical rating
organizations). The Fed's policy is under review.

[79] The Obama administration also proposes to scrutinize the operations of
bank holding companies such as Citigroup and JPMorgan Chase, insurance con-
glomerates such as AIG, and other financial institutions that are deemed too big
to fail.

Making hedge funds and other institutions more transparent cannot hurt, but hopes that this will resolve the "too interconnected to fail" problem are in my view unrealistic; furthermore, they lose sight of the purpose of supervising financial institutions. They are unrealistic for reasons previously stated:

- First, their regulation will consume scarce regulatory resources, so regulators may end up having even less time for the supervision of the traditionally regulated sphere. Given that the regulation of institutions in the traditional sphere has not been "plain sailing," the increase in the agencies' workload raises concerns.

- Second, effective supervision may require shooting at a moving target. Consider, for instance, highly leveraged speculative funds. These hedge funds'[80] activities—providing hedges, speculating, arbitraging, and so forth—are shared by many other corporations, including "nonfinancial" firms. An effective regulation of hedge funds may well lead other institutions to take on their activities. The proposed reforms would subject any institution to regulatory oversight if it is threatening enough to financial-system stability. But the threat in general depends on a complex set of attributes, of which the size of positions is only one component. (For example, capital, risk management, how derivatives are traded, and correlation of balance sheet risk with that of other institutions are four other components.) No specific criterion for putting financial institutions into the tier 1 group is yet available.

What has to be regulated, in my view, is the exposure of the regulated sphere (defined by the representation hypothesis,[81] which is the need to protect small depositors) to the failure of

[80] Hedge funds and private equity firms do not seek to sell to the public but rather to a clientele of rich individuals and financial institutions. Small depositors do not directly interact with these institutions, but they interact indirectly if commercial banks or insurance companies invest in these funds. In 2006, hedge funds had $1,400 billion under management, and two-thirds of them were located in financial paradises. A useful discussion of the role of hedge funds and related regulatory issues can be found in Bank of France (2007).

[81] See Dewatripont and Tirole (1994) for a more complete discussion of the "representation hypothesis" and why representation works differently in the stock market.

unregulated institutions. Rather than enlarging the scope of regulation, one could make sure that banks, insurance companies, and pension funds do not develop substantial and opaque counterparty exposure to prudentially unregulated institutions.

Hedge funds are obviously risky financial institutions, and there have been a number of failures.[82] But the consequences of these failures are quite varied. LTCM's losses, which were related to its exposure to the 1998 Russian crisis, created an unfortunate systemic risk and the Fed had to organize its rescue by the major creditors, leading to its orderly liquidation in 2000. By contrast, the losses of Amaranth in 2006 in the energy derivatives market (which were larger) posed no systemic risk at all.

THE "PUBLIC DOMAIN" AND THE CONTROL OF SYSTEMIC RISK

Having One's Cake and Eating It Too. Supervisors, central banks, and governments were forced to intervene in financial markets through fiscal bailouts, the purchase (or acceptance as collateral) of toxic products, or simply through monetary policy, so as to rescue failed financial institutions that they did not even regulate (investment banks, AIG's holding company).

The fear of systemic risk has taken center stage in the design of public policy because of the opacity of mutual exposures. Regulators have very little information on the exact nature of OTC contracts. They also lack information about the quality of parties engaged in OTC trading, since some of these parties are not regulated or are regulated by different regulators at home or abroad. It is therefore more or less impossible for regulators to understand and invert the matrix of mutual exposures in the global financial system.

Nonetheless, financial instruments that have gone badly off course in recent times can be socially useful if properly employed and should not be banned just because they have been abused. Indeed, some are vital for the dynamism of the global economy. Although securitization and derivatives render the supervision of the financial system a more complex task and their abuse must be curtailed, these techniques allow for better risk management and greater liquidity for financial institutions if they are used

[82] See Bank of France (2007, 50–51).

properly. Securitization allows "dead capital" to be transformed into "live capital" and assists the financing of the economy. It also allows issuers to diversify. Derivatives, for their part, provide economic agents with the possibility of managing their risk efficiently. More generally, finance plays a fundamental role in developing our economy, and it is more reasonable to develop a debate, necessarily technical, on market failure and regulation than to reject in its entirety the apparatus of modern finance, as some do when they propose to ban OTC markets entirely.[83]

Reforms. Thorough reforms are necessary in order to restore transparency and to prevent the emergence of situations in which public authorities are held hostage by a risk of contagion—and don't even know whether it is real or imagined. Two reforms follow from this reasoning:

> *Transparency of mutual exposures or absence thereof.* Regulators need to have a clear view of the exposure of regulated institutions to the failure of other institutions. As we have noted, they have little information about counterparty risk for the moment. Even financial institutions have only a very partial view of the stability of the financial system (some, for example, did not see the problems of AIG and Lehman coming).[84] Accordingly, there are large benefits for the regulator and markets when trades take place through a clearinghouse that acts as a central counterparty in transactions (being a buyer to the seller and a seller to the buyer, when the two parties have agreed on a contract); this clearinghouse then demands margins from participants and takes on the counterparty risk.
>
> It can be countered that clearinghouses themselves may be too big to fail or else will require an unrealistic level of

---

[83] If it is necessary to respond energetically to regulatory failure and reduce both the frequency and scale of crises, one has to abandon the illusion that every crisis can be prevented. In the same way that someone who has never missed a train must be overly risk averse, an economy without crises would be, without a doubt, performing well below its potential. To avoid crises entirely, one would have to constrain risk taking and innovation, and live for the short term rather than invest for the long term.

[84] See, e.g., Tett (2009, 237).

capital. There are two responses to this argument. First, the argument itself goes to the heart of the problem: if enormous amounts of capital are required to sustain the trading of derivatives, the parties currently involved in these markets impose a substantially underpriced risk on society. Second, clearinghouses are easier to monitor and more stable if trades take place in liquid markets. Marking to market then allows a continuous and reliable adjustment of required margins. This brings me to the second point.

Standardization of products. One important activity of finance is the creation of products suited to the particular needs of clients. Nonetheless, capital requirements should be used to encourage regulated intermediaries to trade in standardized products in exchanges, while unregulated intermediaries are left unconstrained in their OTC trading. Regulated institutions could continue trading in bespoke (custom-made) products, but at higher charges unless a well-capitalized central clearinghouse takes on the counterparty risk.

A number of derivative products are linked to macroeconomic shocks (interest rates, exchange rates, stocks, indexes, commodities, large-scale natural catastrophes) or to the failure of large firms or financial institutions, and are therefore either already standardized or easy to standardize.

The loss of fine tailoring arising from standardization is in my view a second-order cost by comparison with the gain in transparency and concomitant improvement in prudential oversight (besides, as we noted, more precisely shaped products can continue to be traded in OTC markets).[85] The examples of contracts exchanged on the Chicago Board of Trade and the Chicago Mercantile Exchange demonstrate that a centralized and securitized system can converge on a framework of reference contracts that satisfy the need for insurance of many parties without engendering systemic risk.

The benefit of centralizing supply and demand in a centralized exchange demanding sufficient collateral from participants is illustrated by the 2006 insolvency of Amaranth,

[85] Serious thought will have to be given to who decides on the selection of admissible products (a panel of industry participants and regulators?) and who deals with the rewriting of existing contracts.

a large hedge fund dealing especially in term contracts for natural gas on centralized platforms. This failure's lack of impact can be contrasted with the (real) collapse of Lehman and the (averted) collapse of AIG, both of which had large OTC activities.

One can anticipate some fighting by the industry against a forced migration toward standardized products, because nonstandard products command much higher fees and involve a higher put on taxpayer money, as unregulated entities become less likely to be rescued.[86]

Finally, analogies with other clearing and settlement systems may provide some inspiration for regulatory reforms. The problem of the control of mutual exposures has long been dealt with in systems of intraday payments. By analogy, one can for instance imagine generalized, multilateral netting for derivative products in which one financial institution will accept taking a limited risk on the failure of every other financial institution.[87] Also, cross-margining agreements among clearinghouses and multisecurity netting should, whenever feasible, allow market participants to economize on their scarce collateral.

Reconsidering Prudential Regulation

THE CYCLICAL EFFECTS OF REGULATION AND
MARKET VALUE ACCOUNTING

Economic Incentives and Accounting. Traditionally, historic cost accounting (HCA) has been applied to the banking portfolios of institutions, while trading book accounting used market prices. The application of international financial reporting standards (IFRS) has extended fair value accounting[88] to part of banking portfolios.

---

[86] The value of this put does not come at the time of the bailout but rather before, as the financial market keeps lending to the distressed institution, giving it a chance to recover.

[87] The possibility of combining the virtues of the gross (such as Fedwire) and the net with bilateral lines of credit (such as CHIPS) is modeled in Rochet and Tirole (1996).

[88] Fair value (or mark-to-market) accounting generally means accounting that uses market prices, whether real or reconstructed, as contrasted with accounting

The defects of historical value accounting are well known. The value initially given to assets may have over time little relation to their real value, creating an important lack of transparency.[89] Certainly, when using historical value accounting, firms are supposed to make provisions for assets that they know to be overvalued by their current accounting value. But the firm has a great deal of room for maneuver in determining the provisions that it really has to make. Institutions subject to HCA routinely retain overvalued assets at their historical value on the balance sheet and sell those that have gained in value,[90] but of course the inverse could well be desirable.[91]

Market value accounting, on the other hand, does have a clear economic logic. First, ex post, it allows those monitoring the firm (board of directors, short-term creditors deciding whether or not to renew their loans, banking regulators, and so on) to form a clear idea of the losses incurred. They thereby acquire information about the performance of the firm's managers and also can prevent behaviors harmful to the firm. On this latter point, it is well known that the managers of firms that are in distress have strong incentives to take major risks (to the detriment of the firm) in a desperate attempt to keep their jobs or to restore the value of stock options that have become "out of the money." Managers may also become entangled in a strategy that

---

that uses historical values or amortized cost. Fair value accounting does not necessitate the existence of liquid and deep markets. For example, American generally accepted accounting principles (GAAP) distinguish three levels: (1) market price, (2) modeled price created on the basis of observable data, and (3) modeled price using more subjective data. (International standards have a more complex, but similar, taxonomy.) For financial institutions, level 1 represents, on average, 25 percent of assets in fair value accounting; level 2, 69 percent; and level 3, 6 percent (International Monetary Fund 2008). For more information on fair value accounting and its consequences, see Matherat (2008).

[89] Opponents of historical value accounting often point to the cases of American S&Ls in the 1980s and Japanese banks in the 1990s.

[90] For an analysis of behavior in gains trading and a comparison of the two accounting systems, see, e.g., Dewatripont and Tirole (1994).

[91] Partly because managers have shown a greater aptitude for managing the assets that have increased in value, and also because selling assets that have decreased in value imposes a contraction of the balance sheet where there is a preponderance of assets overvalued by historical cost accounting.

turns out to be a bad one, in the hope that things will eventually work out and "prove" that they were right.

Market value accounting also provides ex ante incentives to make good investments. Knowing that the firm will be obliged to reduce the size of its balance sheet in case of loss, its managers will necessarily pay more attention to the return on assets.

Yet, market value accounting can violate the principle that managers should be accountable only for events under their control, not for those that are outside their control.[92] These last events include macroeconomic shocks that have not been hedged.

Although market valuation is more reliable than historical valuation when markets are well developed, markets may quickly switch from liquid to illiquid; bad news may engender adverse selection and freeze markets. Furthermore, the macroeconomic effects of market value accounting had been underestimated before the recent financial crisis. Even a small fall in the price of assets (for example, housing prices) can snowball: the financial intermediaries whose balance sheets are hit must recapitalize so as to keep with prudential rules. If they are unsuccessful in raising new equity from investors, they sell assets, putting downward pressure on prices, which in turn leads all financial intermediaries into a downward spiral of undercapitalization and asset defeasance.

Faced with criticisms of the effects of market value accounting on economic activity, the international agencies for accounting standards (FASB, IASB) argue that macroeconomic stabilization is no part of the mission of accountancy. This raises the question (to which we now turn) of whether the procyclicality of current regulation should not be addressed in a different way.

Capital Requirements. The principle of invariance of prudential capital requirements through the cycle is being revisited. The Basel Committee announced on November 20, 2008, that it will envisage mandating provisioning during phases of expansion. Similarly, the U.S. Treasury's June 2009 proposal states that capital and liquidity requirements would possibly be tied to the

---

[92] In economic jargon this is called the "sufficient statistic principle"; it was developed by Holmström (1979).

economic cycle. Earlier, the principle of invariant prudential policy through the cycle had already been undermined in Spain, where the regulator required banks, through "dynamic provisioning," de facto to exceed the minimum solvency ratio during the boom preceding the subprime crisis. Finally, we should note that in many countries regulators use "filters,"[93] which allow banks to smooth capital gains and losses over time.[94]

But countercyclical solvency ratios (that is, higher capital requirements during booms) until recently were taboo. It was (correctly) argued that a regulator runs the risk of being subjected to intense lobbying if it has discretionary powers to adjust the solvency ratio.[95] There are, however, good theoretical reasons in favor of countercyclical capital adequacy requirements:

• First, a shortage of banking capital goes hand in hand with a contraction of credit (a "credit crunch"), increased yield spreads between bank loans and risk-free assets, and serious economic difficulties for firms with fragile balance sheets, such as small and medium enterprises, which are dependent on borrowing from banks.

• Second, public policy has to assist the financial system during periods of liquidity shortage:[96] for example, the relaxation of constraints on solvency during such periods is one way to render such assistance, alongside monetary policy.[97]

---

[93] Such filters are not internationally standardized. For more about filters, see Matherat (2008).

[94] Such smoothing no doubt suffers from the discretionary aspect of the filters.

[95] Lobbying can in part be mitigated by the independence of the regulator from the political process, on the one hand, and by rules that define a recession, on the other.

[96] The more so for liquidity shocks that have a low probability of occurrence (so that it is very costly for the private sector to set funds aside against such events).

[97] These two arguments are developed in Holmström and Tirole (1997, 1998), respectively. The book I wrote with Mathias Dewatripont (Dewatripont and Tirole 1994) suggests a reduction in the procyclical character of regulation by introducing deposit insurance premiums that are themselves procyclical (that is, increase at the top of the cycle). This suggestion would be even more advantageous for a fair value accounting system, for such a system is naturally more volatile than one based on historic values.

The Articulation of Accounting with Capital Requirements.
The principle of fair value accounting has itself been undermined
by several policy moves, such as a provision of the Paulson Plan
authorizing regulators to suspend use of market value accounting. Similarly, on October 15, 2008, the International Accounting Standards Board (with the agreement of European regulators) moved toward the American practices of generally accepted
accounting principles and accepted the reclassification of some
assets from trading book to banking book, de facto boosting the
evaluation of balance sheets. More precisely, the IFRS standards
distinguish among three classes of assets: (1) "available for trade,"
recorded at market values both on the profit and loss account
and on the balance sheet,[98] (2) "available for sale," recorded at
market value solely on the balance sheet,[99] and (3) "held to maturity," which are not recorded at market value.[100] The Board
allowed in particular reclassifications from (2) to (3).

My current view on this matter is that, in spite of some important defects, market value accounting is vital to an accurate
understanding of the state of a firm's balance sheet. Its perverse
macroeconomic effects can to some extent be limited by setting
up a countercyclical capital requirement or dynamic provisioning for financial intermediaries.

Accountancy is not a simple financial thermometer; it is not
neutral with respect to economic behavior. Economists will have
to burrow into the detail of macroprudential monitoring, a
major challenge for regulation. For example, the economic theory of bubbles suggests that an overvaluation of assets will need
to be reflected in capital requirements for two reasons. First, the
bubble may burst, so it has to be viewed as a highly risky asset.
Second, it in a sense "bursts at the wrong time." The collapse
of a bubble involves a loss of both wealth and liquidity for the
economy and paves the way to recession. The asset has lost value

[98] Balance sheet accounting has a direct impact on regulatory equity. Profit
and loss accounting matters through the information so conveyed, as it affects
the market's valuation of the firm, or its capacity to borrow.

[99] With some exceptions (large drops in share prices can also be registered in
the profit and loss account).

[100] If an asset in this category is sold before expiry of its term, the whole portfolio has to be restructured (the "tainting" rule).

precisely at a time at which cash is badly needed. Such theoretical considerations[101] qualify the use of a technique, fair value accounting, that is otherwise justified.

Clearly, the proposal to make capital requirements vary through the cycle might hamper the international standardization of capital requirements. It also would be less attractive in case of a symbiotic relationship between the financial sector and its regulators. There is also the problem that economic and banking cycles do not necessarily coincide. Economic consideration of these issues is therefore called for, determining how it might be possible to define countercyclical requirements for equity in a way that will not be too open to manipulation.

Finally, economists need to turn their attention to the linkage between accounting and the duration of asset holding: Should an institution with long-term liabilities (insurance companies, long-term investors) be affected by changes in market price in the same way as institutions with shorter liabilities?

THE REGULATION OF LIQUIDITY

At present there is no uniform treatment of liquidity regulation, whether through the Basel accords or within, say, Europe. The prudential regulation of liquidity can be justified in the same way as that of solvency, in terms of (a) the protection of small savers (or taxpayers) on the one hand, and (b) the avoidance of systemic effects on the other. On this latter point, we should note that liquidity is subject to network effects, for two reasons: first, banks are mutually exposed in, for instance, interbank markets and derivatives markets. A lack of liquidity for one has repercussions for the others. Another factor of such interdependence, on the asset side of the balance sheet, is that banks often count on the sale of similar assets to satisfy their need for liquidity; but if this need for liquidity is brought about by bad macroeconomic news, the secondary market will overflow with sell orders and will see a substantial fall in price (a fire sale), and so banks will not be able to count on the level of desired liquidity.[102]

---

[101] See Farhi and Tirole (2010) for a theoretical model that validates these points.

[102] If liquid assets, as they should, carry a low yield and therefore are costly to hoard, they presumably will be held for the purpose of future acquisitions only if

It is notoriously difficult to construct a good measure of the liquidity of a firm or of a financial intermediary. On the asset side of the balance sheet ("market liquidity"), liquidity depends on the ability to sell securities (Treasury bonds, certificates of deposit, shares, bonds, etc.) and other assets (securitization) when needed without incurring too great a loss in value. On the liability side ("funding liquidity"), liquidity depends on the prospect of quickly raising funds under acceptable conditions (short-term liabilities in the wholesale market, etc.). Liquidity also depends on reputation, which affects the capacity both to dispose of assets and to raise new funds.

These difficulties underlie the frequent use of stress tests not only by institutions for internal purposes, but more and more by regulators. Stress tests of course are only as good as the data that are fed into them.[103] Prior to the crisis, simulations of balance sheet evolution tended to use distributions based on short time series that vastly underestimated tail risk. The calculation of value at risk (VaR) was done by reference to good years, and little macroeconomic diagnosis was performed in anticipation of shocks to come. Obviously, regulators, industry, and academic economists need to refine their models substantially so as to get a more accurate picture of liquidity and solvency. The confluence of two economic fields—prudential regulation (usually treated purely in terms of microeconomics) and macroeconomic policy (which has for a long time ignored the phenomenon of imperfect financial markets)—requires new thinking.

More generally, developing a better understanding of what drives illiquidity at the institution's and aggregate levels should stand high on the agenda of economists and policy makers.

the secondary market price is expected to embody a discount relative to the primary market price; Allen and Gale (e.g., in their 2005 paper) call this arbitrage condition "cash-in-the-market pricing." Recent research has investigated the welfare cost of fire sales: see in particular Lorenzoni (2008).

[103] Bebchuk (2009) is very critical of the stress tests conducted last spring by the Obama administration, which have led to a number of banks being allowed to repay the capital injected into them by U.S. authorities. In particular, he argues that losses on loans maturing after 2010 were ignored. He further argues that the banks' ability to raise new equity capital isn't proof that the banks that passed the stress tests are adequately capitalized, as equity reflects only the upside potential, not the downside.

THE REGULATION OF SOLVENCY

The calculation of equity requirements will always be evolving, regulators playing a catch-up game with regulated institutions. Because leverage is key to return on equity, the latter have an incentive to minimize their use of capital and thereby to enjoy greater freedom. Their taking advantage of the loose capital requirements on liquidity support to off-balance-sheet vehicles is a case in point.

Beyond the technical (but highly important!) question of risk measurement, there is the question of what the Basel rules are seeking to accomplish.[104] These rules focus on the risk of default on the part of a given bank. This approach raises two questions: Is the probability of default the proper object of investigation? Also, is it legitimate to focus on each bank in isolation?

Regarding the first question, we can note that the cost of failure for the depositors, the deposit insurance fund, and the taxpayers is the product of the probability of failure and the average loss in the event of failure; this fact is acknowledged in the concept of "loss given default." That said, the loss given default is highly endogenous; it can be made extremely high, as when the bank concentrates the risks in some extreme events of low probability. This limits of the concept of VaR in stress tests used by regulators.[105]

In answering the second question, we note that a bank's failure does not have the same consequences during a period of crisis as it does during an otherwise calm period. First, such a failure has a greater chance of having a systemic impact if other banks are simultaneously affected by a macroeconomic shock and therefore may become undercapitalized; the interconnection among banks, either directly through mutual exposures or indirectly through the phenomenon of fire sales, then means that the bank's failure may trigger domino effects.[106] Also, correlation of positions

---

[104] See chapter 3.

[105] For other criticisms of VaR, see chapter 3.

[106] Of course, the exact impact depends on how the authorities react to a bank's failure: whether they bail it out and force some contraction in the size of the balance sheet or just let the bank fail, and whether they wipe out wholesale creditors.

across banks puts monetary authorities in a bind. This all suggests that capital requirements should be higher the more the bank's failure is likely to coincide with (or be driven by) macroeconomic shocks and other banks' failure. Again, this suggests complementing the traditional microbased regulation with macroprudential regulation.

Other Reforms

COMPENSATION

At the G20 meeting in London (April 2, 2009) leaders endorsed the Financial Stability Forum's (2009) recommendations on compensation. More generally, regulatory proposals have been made to better align managerial incentives with those of shareholders and society.

Policies Limiting Incentive Payments and Requiring the Use of Restricted Stock. There is a consensus,[107] at least as a matter of principle (implementation of this principle is a much more complex issue), that longer-term incentives reduce risk taking and are more appropriate than standard compensation packages.

In the United States, both the TARP (2008) and stimulus (2009) bills require that incentives for "unnecessary and excessive risk taking" be removed in institutions that benefit from TARP funds. The stimulus bill limits incentive pay for executives of these banks to at most one-third of compensation. Furthermore, these bills specify that incentive pay should come in the form of restricted stock. France adopted a bonus-malus system,[108] in which bank managers and employees will not receive the compensation attached to good performance if the performance later degrades; such a regulation mandates a sufficient vesting period for bonuses.[109] By the same logic, it has been proposed that if the financial institution goes bankrupt, the pool of deferred bonuses should be transferred to the deposit insurance fund to help recoup some

---

[107] See, e.g., Bernanke (2009).

[108] On August 25, 2009.

[109] The vesting period is the period of time before shares are owned unconditionally by the employee.

of society's cost. Such regulations, in my view, go in the right direction, even though their implementation is not always straight-forward.[110]

As an aside, it is unclear to me why the American bills' provisions, or any rule that would be deemed more efficient, should apply only to beneficiaries of TARP funds and not more broadly to regulated/depository institutions that benefit from deposit insurance and/or may be bailed out by the government. Put differently, the oversight of compensation should be forward-looking and not single out institutions that use TARP funds.

The focus on restricted stock reflects the need to provide managers and employees with long-term incentives. For top officers, it implies that shares cannot be unloaded quickly. More generally, and as a matter of theory, the Financial Stability Forum (2009) correctly notes that the extent to which compensation should be deferred depends on the time horizon of the risk, that is, on the speed at which information about performance accrues. The "day of reckoning" may vary substantially depending on the type of activity.

The Financial Stability Forum (2009) further calls for an adjustment of compensation to risk.[111] This also makes theoretical sense. The implementation of this principle, however, is very complex (as we know from the attempts to define risk-adjusted returns for comparing the performance of fund managers) in that it requires a good statistical model of the employee's activity. Furthermore, what is risky for an employee may not be risky for her institution (think of a hedging operation), and vice versa. The implementation of this principle is information intensive.

---

[110] Bonus-malus systems need to keep individual records in some units of account (profits, evaluation by a supervisor), in the same way that funds keep track of past performances of their employees in high-water-mark schemes (in which, when the value of investments decreases, fund managers must increase the value above the previous high in order to receive performance fees again).

[111] "Two employees who generate the same short-run profit but take different amounts of risk on behalf of their firm should not be treated the same by the compensation system. In general, both quantitative measures and human judgment should play a role in determining risk adjustments. Risk adjustments should account for all types of risk, including difficult-to-measure risks such as liquidity risk, reputation risk and cost of capital."

Compensation Oversight. "Oversight" can be private and public. The recent crisis reignited the old and broader debate on "say on pay," that is, on nonbinding shareholder resolutions on managerial compensation schemes as a way to align managerial incentives with the interests of shareholders.[112]

But more to the point for financial regulation reforms, are the measures taken to reinforce external supervision of executive compensation in regulated segments. Banking supervisors should have a say in the structure of compensation to the extent that the form of compensation has a strong impact on the risk behavior of regulated entities—which they are meant to monitor (a principle emphasized in Financial Stability Forum 2009). Several countries have named "pay czars" (Kenneth Feinberg in the United States, Michel Camdessus in France) to oversee the compensation of the most highly paid banking executives.

But there are limits to what direct regulation by the state can do. First, hubris can play as big a part as financial gains in generating dysfunctional behavior (French observers need only recall the oversized egos of those embroiled in the recent Société Générale scandal, in which a trader, Jerome Kerviel, lost €5 billion, and the Crédit Lyonnais debacle in the early 1990s). Second, government regulations can be circumvented, leading to significant inefficiencies (benefits in kind, retirement packages, options, a choice of governance favorable to managers, and so on). Finally, if their compensation is limited by regulation, the best managers and traders might move to hedge funds or other unregulated agents or go abroad.

Therefore it seems more constructive to supervise the way the regulated private sector revises its compensation packages and makes them more oriented to the long run,[113] and to require, in

---

[112] This does not preclude the traditional form of compensation oversight by the board, the necessity of which is noted by the Financial Stability Forum (2009). See also Bebchuk and Spamann (2009) for a discussion of "say on pay" votes of shareholders.

[113] The limits of this argument are well known. Long-term remuneration plans (stock option plans in particular vary widely) are systematically renegotiated if the incentives they create either cease to exist or become perverse with the emergence of bad news.

conformity with the second "pillar" of Basel II,[114] an increase in bank capital if these schemes keep creating pressure toward short-termism and heightened risk taking.

Monitoring by "compensation czars" will serve a purpose, I believe, but even a competent and well-intentioned supervisor of compensation practices will have limited knowledge and ability to counter the institutions' natural inclination toward short-termist and risk-friendly incentive schemes. This is why monitoring compensation is at best a complement to the other measures regulators need to take to curb such behaviors. For example, I would expect measures reducing the use of OTC markets and forcing protection to be arranged through standardized products traded in exchanges to do more to reduce trader bonuses than direct regulation of bonuses.

CREDIT-RATING AGENCIES

The crisis once more implicated credit-rating agencies. Such agencies play a central role in modern finance, notifying both individuals and regulators of the risks affecting a variety of financial instruments. Banks and other financial intermediaries have a great deal to lose from a loss of trust in rating agencies, as this would lead to increased capital requirements.

A number of reforms are contemplated. In April 2009, the G20 followed up on European impetus to impose constraints on credit-rating agencies.[115] The U.S. Treasury's June 2009 proposal offers to subject rating agencies to tougher disclosure standards.

[114] This second section of the 2004 Basel II accord (supervisory review process) authorizes regulators and others to raise equity requirements.

[115] "As a rule, all credit rating agencies that would like their credit ratings to be used in the EU will need to apply for registration. The applications will be submitted to the Committee of European Securities Regulators (CESR) and decided upon in a consensual manner by the relevant securities regulators grouped in a college. The college of regulators will also be involved in the day-to-day supervision of credit rating agencies. Specific, albeit sufficiently exacting, treatment is envisaged and may be extended, on a case-by-case basis, to credit rating agencies operating exclusively from non-EU jurisdictions provided that their countries of origin have established regulatory and supervisory frameworks as stringent as the one now put in place in the EU. Registered credit rating agencies will have to comply with rigorous rules to make sure (1) that ratings are not affected by conflicts of interest, (2) that credit rating agencies remain vigilant on the quality of the rating methodology and the ratings, and (3) that credit rating agencies act in

It is sometimes argued that there is no need to rely on credit-rating agencies and that it is up to financial institutions themselves to make their own judgments.[116] This argument has plausibility given the poor performance of credit-rating agencies in the subprime crisis,[117] and it fits with the idea that one should always have a wide range of independent views.

This argument has limitations, however.

- First, it is very expensive to measure risk well when a security is issued, or subsequently to revise a rating. Indeed, competition among the existing credit-rating agencies is

a transparent manner. The Regulation also includes an effective surveillance regime whereby regulators will supervise credit rating agencies. New rules include the following:

Credit rating agencies may not provide advisory services.

They will not be allowed to rate financial instruments if they do not have sufficient quality information to base their ratings on.

They must disclose the models, methodologies and key assumptions on which they base their ratings.

They must differentiate the ratings of more complex products by adding a specific symbol.

They will be obliged to publish an annual transparency report.

They will have to create an internal function to review the quality of their ratings.

They should have at least two independent directors on their boards whose remuneration cannot depend on the business performance of the rating agency. They will be appointed for a single term of office which can be no longer than five years. They can only be dismissed in case of professional misconduct. At least one of them should be an expert in securitisation and structured finance.

The new rules are largely based on the standards set in the International Organisation of Securities Commissions (IOSCO) code. The Regulation imposes rules which have a legally binding character." (European Commission press release, April 23, 2009)

[116]For example, "The Committee recommends that investors conduct their own due diligence on structured products, with respect to their investment mandates, horizons, and risk appetites, and not rely solely on ratings in making their investment decisions" (Institute of International Finance 2008, 16).

[117]Not to mention the dotcom bubble, the Enron and WorldCom scandals, and the sovereign funds crises, where in each instance credit-rating agencies, as in the subprime case, very markedly underestimated risks and adjusted their ratings only shortly before the collapse, in what were known as "express-train downgrades."

very limited in part because information provision is a kind of "natural monopoly,"[118] so it is hard to image that hundreds or thousands of institutions would come to their own independent conclusions about the risks attached to a huge number of securities. Independent judgment of those acquiring securities applies above all to a few large and very sophisticated players.

• Second, there is the issue of regulatory gaming. Ratings are, like market value accounting, one way in which regulators make sense of the reality of the balance sheet of a bank, an insurance company, a broker, or a pension fund. Regulated institutions have a strong incentive to overvalue for regulatory purposes the securities they hold; relying on their "assessment" for the determination of capital (in the spirit of internal modeling) creates hazards.

This leads me to the major argument regarding the need for at least a minimum of regulation of credit-rating agencies: that over time they have become "auxiliary regulators" and as such make a considerable amount of money. The capital demanded of regulated institutions (banks, insurance companies, brokers, pension funds) is seriously reduced when they hold highly rated securities.[119] The privilege enjoyed by credit-rating agencies should be associated with regulatory oversight of their activities. (This argument does not apply to the activities of credit-rating agencies outside the domain of prudential regulation, however.)

Different approaches can be explored to make ratings more relevant: increasing competition in the rating market,[120] eliminating conflicts of interest, defining best practices, developing measurements of forecasting quality, recording the past performance

[118] "Natural monopoly" means that the collection of information by a single entity (or, if there are mistakes, by a couple of entities) is definitely cost-efficient. Incentive and market-power considerations, however, may call for more competition than there is currently among credit-rating agencies. (The lack of competition is also partly due to regulatory decisions.)

[119] Franke and Krahnen (2008) note that, contrary to the theory that banking institutions will, for reasons related to incentives, hold tranches of less highly rated debt, in fact regulated institutions retain or buy the majority of senior or super-senior tranches. The role of credit-rating agencies in determining capital requirements is without doubt the cause of this behavior.

[120] There were initially three NRSROs in 1975 and only eight in 2008 (source: DefaultRisk.com, April 11, 2008).

of each agency in a central register, and creating an international regulatory agency for credit-rating agencies that would, in consort with the prudential regulators, define accredited practices for calculating the capital of banks, insurance companies, and other regulated financial intermediaries.

To current proposals, I would add the standardization of ratings. Just appending "sf" to a rating of a structured finance product does not suffice.[121] A given rating must mean the same thing whether the liability involves local government, a firm, or a portfolio of mortgages; however, a collateralized debt obligation with a Baa rating had a probability of default eight times greater than a corporate bond with the same rating. Similarly, given the same rating, local government liabilities have a probability of default much lower than those recently generated by structured finance.[122] Rating agencies should be required to standardize their assessments so that investors and regulators know what kind of risks they are exposing themselves to.

By contrast, other proposals directed to the oversight of rating agencies seem less appropriate, or at least in need of much more detailed consideration. Some have suggested that the information given by issuers to credit-rating agencies should be made public, allowing sophisticated investors to reproduce or refute agencies' predictions. Issuers might then hold back more information, in the knowledge that information given to rating agencies would be diffused more widely in the market.

It has also been suggested that ratings agencies be paid by investors, not by issuers, in order to reduce conflicts of interest. The argument stems from the principle that those who are under scrutiny must not bribe the scrutinizers.[123] Yet the question is not who pays, but rather who decides on the identity of the scrutinizer:

[121] The reform proposals of the Securities and Exchange Commission, the International Organization of Securities Commissions, the Financial Stability Forum, and the Institute of International Finance suggest that ratings for complex products be given a suffix, for instance "sf" for structured finance. See also the European Commission's April 2009 press release mentioned earlier.

[122] One interesting statistic is that of downgrades between July 2007 and June 2008. According to Bloomberg, agencies reduced the ratings for structured products 145,899 times, compared to 1,445 times for corporate bonds. See, for example, Commission Staff (2008) for details about ratings revisions.

[123] But see Kovbasyuk (2010), who argues that contingent payments by issuers to rating agencies improve welfare provided that the contracts between issuers

the fact that a student pays to take an entry-level examination or a driving test poses no special problem. Besides, it is not clear that returning to the system of "user pays" that prevailed a long time ago would be workable; the current system of "issuer pays" reflects the fact that information is a public good; if an investor acquires the rating of a security, this rating can be freely made available to all other investors, hence depriving the rating agency of its source of income.

Making the methods used in the calculation of ratings more transparent is also often suggested. Given the weak connection between ratings and outcomes in the case of structured products, this is a tempting proposition. It seems reasonable to create a body defining the standards and following up the activities and methodologies of credit-rating agencies whenever ratings are used for prudential purposes. But thought must also be given to the possible perverse effects of this approach. First, real transparency will reduce the role of subjective factors in the creation of ratings. Second, if confidentiality is not guaranteed and thus intellectual property not protected, rating agencies could be discouraged from developing new evaluative methodologies.

REGULATION OF SECURITIZATION:
MINIMUM STAKE AND REPUTATION RISK

It has been proposed that securitization be regulated directly by obliging issuers to retain a minimum stake of their issues on their balance sheets. The economic rationale for such a measure is quite plain: moral hazard is reduced by the issuer retaining a stake. Partial securitization therefore promotes accountability.

Implementation of this principle is riddled with pitfalls, however.[124] The stake to be retained is far from being uniform and depends both on what securities are issued and the way in which they are issued. First, some activities are much riskier than others. For instance, in public-sector outsourcing, a contractor to whom a reliable local body guarantees a stream of future revenues can, without presenting much loss of accountability, securitize more

and rating agencies are public (Kovbasyuk shows that the conclusions are rather different if those contracts are not transparent).

[124] The same difficulties apply to the otherwise desirable differentiation of capital requirements on the buying side of securitized products.

or less the entire revenue stream. By contrast, holders of debt subject to significant moral hazard in monitoring the borrowers should retain a major part of such debt on their balance sheets, a rule that clearly was infringed in the case of subprime loans.

The quality of the securitization process is also relevant. To give a hypothetical example, let us imagine that credit-rating agencies are able (and have an incentive) to perfectly estimate the quality of a securitized portfolio. To require the issuer to retain a minimum percentage of the portfolio on its balance sheet would then result in economic losses, since the issuer will already be held fully accountable by the impact of his decisions on the market price of the securitized portfolio. More generally, the minimum economically justifiable percentage depends of the quality of the rating process, on the reputation of the investment bank carrying out the securitization, and on every other factor of reduction of informational asymmetries between issuers and purchasers.

Moreover, the incentive effect arising from the issuer's retained stake holds only so long as the issuer does not cover the corresponding risk through a derivatives operation with a third party. This is not a new argument: in like fashion, the incentive properties of managerial compensation packages (for instance, the holding of shares or of stock options) are compromised if the managers secretly insure themselves against the related risk (for example, by short selling a number of shares equal to the quantity that the remuneration scheme specifies has to be retained). And in fact managers sometimes get caught engaging in this kind of fraud. It is likewise obvious that the regulation of securitization must require issuers not to cover the risk that they agree to retain.

Overall, it is hard to do better than the very mild reform envisioned by the July 22, 2009, Treasury proposal or the European decision in the matter—namely, requiring the issuer to retain a stake equal to at least 5 percent of the issue—because it is difficult to know in the abstract how much "skin in the game" issuers should keep.[125]

---

[125] On the idea that one size does not fit all, see Fender and Mitchell (2009), which also shows that the originator is not always best incentivized through the holding of the equity tranche: under certain circumstances, having the originator

Finally, as we have noted, issuers sometimes perceive an obligation to assume losses of securitized products that they are no longer legally obliged to cover, in order to preserve their reputations.[126] Reputation risk is not covered by capital requirements. I therefore propose the following policy: a regulated institution, having disposed of risk associated with a securitized product, should be prevented from providing assistance to the corresponding product or vehicle or else incur a sanction by the regulator. In other words, the regulator could be employed as a commitment mechanism in the wasteful signaling game between the issuer and the market. The alternative, instituting a capital charge for reputation risk, seems complex, as there are no good measures of reputation risk. This proposal differs from, but is similar in spirit to, Basel II–compatible reforms. In particular, the Basel Committee on Banking Supervision in a consultative document (2009) proposed that the risk arising from the potential provision of implicit support be considered part of the pillar 2 process (i.e., the supervisory review process).[127]

DISSEMINATION OF BEST PRACTICES AND CODES
OF BANKING CONDUCT

Many international bodies have defined codes of good conduct.[128] Such codes are useful for two reasons. First, they promote discussion and can play a role in the diffusion of best practices. Second, they remind managers of particular risks that they

---

retain a mezzanine slice can elicit more monitoring than retention of the equity tranche.

[126] The same may happen with REITs (real estate investment trusts), in-house hedge funds, money market funds, or any other entity that is sponsored by the institution. The institution may be tempted to support the value of shares even when it has no such legal obligation.

[127] The Basel II accord defines three pillars. The other two are pillar 1 (minimum capital requirements) and pillar 3 (market discipline).

[128] For example, the Institute of International Finance (2008) makes a long list of recommendations for financial institutions. As an illustration, it recommends reaffirming the responsibility of the CEO in the management of risk, the adoption of an integrated approach to risk and its concentration at the level of the firm, the verification that stress tests and liquidity measures reflect a number of considerations (such as the risk of not being able to refinance by selling or securitizing assets—"pipeline and warehousing risk"), and the adoption of incentive compensation (with performance measures adjusted to take account of risk).

might forget. In some cases, such codes can also change norms internal to the firm, by for instance reinforcing the prestige of some jobs such as that of "chief risk officer."

Nonetheless, the gains that we can expect from such recommendations will always be limited. Agents in the financial sector, like all other agents in society, respond to the incentives with which they are faced. Recommendations that run counter to their private interest amount to pious hopes.[129] One needs to take with a grain of salt proposals based mainly on the observance of codes of good conduct.

Regulatory Infrastructure and International Banking Coordination

NATIONAL INFRASTRUCTURES

The crisis will accelerate thinking about regulatory infrastructure: on the possibility of regulators taking drastic corrective action in advance of a bank's closure,[130] on the coordination between authorities in different countries, and also of course on domestic regulatory coordination.[131]

THE HANDLING OF INSOLVENT TRANSNATIONAL GROUPS

The problem of transnational groups is an especially pressing one and requires greater coordination of authorities in different countries. Regulation (supervision and compliance with capital adequacy requirements obey the "home country rule") and crisis

---

[129] For example, the recommendation that issuers devote as much attention to the selection of credits they intend to securitize as to those they will keep on their balance sheet clearly fails to distinguish private from social interest; it is hardly surprising that empirical evidence shows that this recommendation is honored more in the breach than in the observance.

[130] At the date of this writing the Obama administration was working on the issue of resolution authority for systemically important players. Resolution problems are also important in Europe.

[131] On this last point, it has often been pointed out that regulation in the United States was hampered by overlapping jurisdictions. We mentioned the issue of regulatory shopping. Another issue is accountability: for instance, the Fed, insurance regulators, and banking regulators all had a say on undercapitalized monolines. The June 2009 Treasury proposal includes a number of changes in the regulatory structure.

management (bailouts or the acceptance of an institution's insolvency, repurchase of toxic assets, etc.) are textbook cases of "games with externalities." According to the Basel Accords, each country is responsible for supervising banks in terms of their consolidated global activities. But it is important to align the incentives on individual states with those of the international community as a whole. Choices made by authorities in one country regarding capital requirements or insolvency have an impact on investors, counterparties, and deposit insurance funds in other countries. Despite all the talk about international cooperation, we should expect free riding. The recent example of guarantees for all bank deposits[132] to attract deposits from foreign banking systems is a textbook case of "every man for himself."

The defense of national self-interest has a particular impact on bank bailouts. Through mergers and internal development, European banks have increased their cross-border activities, and this trend will continue. At least since the rescue of the Italian Banco Ambrosiano in 1982 (the initial bailout plan not including the bank's subsidiary in Luxembourg), authorities have been unhappy about the coordination of bailout plans but have not come up with a satisfactory solution. On January 4, 2010, Iceland refused to compensate Britain and the Netherlands (whose deposit insurance funds had to oblige by the deposit insurance promises) for the costs they incurred following the collapse of the Icesave bank in 2008. It can also be anticipated that states will provide too little support. For example, the incentive for Switzerland or the Netherlands to rescue a large bank whose business is mostly abroad is likely to be inadequate unless there is a larger-scale international negotiation involved. Finally, in bank bailout operations, restrictions are sometimes put on the support given to the bank's foreign subsidiaries. Likewise, Lehman Brothers, protected by Chapter 11 of the U.S. bankruptcy law, repatriated the liquidity of its foreign subsidiaries to the

---

[132] The choice made at the beginning of October 2008 by Ireland, Austria, Germany, Denmark, Hungary, Slovakia, and Slovenia to extend insurance to all deposits could be viewed as unfair competition for wholesale deposits at a time when there was a shortage of liquidity.

United States.[133] American ring-fencing is a good example of protectionism at work.

Generally, it is better to agree on a framework for cooperation ex ante, "behind the veil of ignorance," than to seek to do so ex post, when governments are mainly concerned with the reaction of domestic public opinion.

An Integrated Approach . . . . Let us start with the coordination of prudential supervision, for example, in the European context (a number of points carry over to other or broader contexts). A centralization of this kind would facilitate the creation of a considerable pool of talent, since it seems unlikely that the supervisory agencies of twenty-seven countries would individually be able to field all the necessary expertise in the face of strong competition from the private sector for the best talent. And centralization mainly would take a European rather than member state perspective.[134]

Locating this European regulator within the ECB would have two additional benefits. First, it would improve coordination between supervision and monetary policy. Second, the independence of the ECB would underwrite the independence of regulation (alternatives are available to achieve this).

In contrast with the United States (where the Fed and the Treasury have worked hand in hand in the recent crisis), the absence of a European Treasury is a problem. In spite of the recent experience in the rescues of Fortis and Dexia,[135] one should not expect

---

[133] It is possible, moreover, that the international character of exposures to Lehman Brothers played a role in the decision to handle its failure differently from that of Bear Stearns.

[134] Creating a European supervisor (or, at the world level, a "World Financial Organization" or, more modestly, a global supervisory body, as some have proposed) is acceptable only insofar as this supervisor is provided with an incentive to anticipate problems, to adopt an economic approach to regulation, and to avoid becoming a bureaucracy. It should not be a political arena in which representatives of governments are more preoccupied with domestic opinion in their countries than with the mission of the organization. For a theoretical discussion of the organization of international bodies, see Tirole (2002, chapter 7).

[135] Again, there is controversy over whether either of these rescues was conducted under suitable conditions. In the case of Fortis, the seizure of local assets of the bank by the Dutch authorities (who had not appreciated that they were not the lead regulator for Fortis following the purchase of the Dutch bank ABN

things always to be resolved by international negotiation, as each country has an incentive to hide information in difficult times and later to underestimate its responsibility in the problem so as to minimize its contribution to the bailout (Freixas 2003).

The idea has at times been advanced of creating a fund at the European level to provide a rapid response for insolvent European banks.[136] Schoenmaker and Goodhart (2006) consider this solution unrealistic and ineffective.[137] It is unrealistic because those countries with sound banking systems will probably not accept implicit transfers to countries whose banks are more fragile or whose regulators are more lax. It is ineffective because it mutualizes losses and therefore restricts incentives to adopt a policy of strict regulatory supervision.

Even though any form of pan-European fiscalism runs up against the question of implicit transfers between states, Goodhart and Schoenmaker's reasoning actually offers another argument in favor of centralized regulation. The latter would dispose of an important cause of heterogeneity across states, namely that associated with different qualities of regulatory oversight.

Last, whether centralization is accomplished or not, it would be desirable to create some uniformity in the resolution mechanism for failing financial institutions. This is by no means an easy task, as countries exhibit a wide heterogeneity of legal forms (common and Roman law, to take the most obvious source of heterogeneity).

. . . Versus a More Decentralized One. In the absence of structures created at the European level, it will no doubt be necessary to reconsider the allocation of responsibilities across countries. Take the case of deposit insurance. At the moment, if a bank defaults, its foreign subsidiaries are covered by the insurance system of the host country, that is, the country within which

---

Amro by Fortis in 2007) seriously hampered the negotiations. In the case of Dexia, shareholders were partially compensated, although they would have received nothing in the event of bankruptcy.

[136] The centralizing agent could be, for instance, the European Investment Bank.

[137] Another useful article on the topic of burden sharing is Herring (2006).

the subsidiary is located.[138] Yet, it would seem normal that the regulator of a bank take responsibility for the costs of bankruptcy in regard to deposit insurance in other countries. One could, for instance, imagine that the state supervising the bank within the framework of "home-host" supervision guarantee retail deposits in its foreign subsidiaries.[139]

TOWARD A NEW INTERNATIONAL FINANCIAL ARCHITECTURE?

In July 1944, representatives of forty-four allied nations met in Bretton Woods, New Hampshire, to design a new international monetary system. There followed the redefinition of commercial and financial rules, the pegging of exchange rates to gold, and the creation of two multilateral organizations: the International Monetary Fund, at the time intended to assist countries faced with disequilibria in their balance of payments; and what is now known as the World Bank.

Financial regulation must be international, just as banks have become over the last thirty years. The elaboration of new rules by international organizations—the Basel Committee for banks, the International Association of Insurance Supervisors for insurance companies, the International Organization of Securities Commissions for securities markets, and the International Accounting Standards Board for accounting standards—has become widely accepted. But the creation of supranational regulatory structures has become increasingly urgent in a world in which institutions and counterparties are truly international. The G20 process illustrates the start of a dialogue. For example, financial havens and tax competition are no longer taboo topics. Let us hope that, past the downturn and with waning public attention to financial issues, the political resolve will remain strong enough to bring about the reforms and build the institutions that will be required to avoid a repetition of this major failure.

[138] For foreign branches of a bank—a more unusual corporate structure—by contrast, the deposit insurance system of the home country in which the company is registered in principle compensates the host country depositors.

[139] In Europe the minimum deposit insurance is €30,000, but the actual level varies greatly from country to country (in France it is €70,000). Australia and New Zealand had no deposit insurance before the crisis, but this is now under review.

CHAPTER 3

The Future of Banking Regulation

Jean-Charles Rochet

The Basel Accords

The Basel Committee on Banking Supervision was created in 1974 on the initiative of the Group of Ten, following the collapse of the German bank Herstatt.[1] Its purpose is to lay down prudential rules applicable to all banks that have a significant international presence. During the 1980s, some members of the committee (especially American and British representatives) were concerned about the frenetic increase in the total assets of Japanese banks, banks that were notoriously undercapitalized and enjoyed an implicit guarantee from the Japanese government in case of failure. In 1988, the committee formulated a set of prudential rules aimed at improving the stability of the international banking system and suppressing distortions arising in competition among countries. These are known as the first Basel Accords, and commonly referred to as Basel I.

These first accords were subject to wide-ranging criticism from both commercial bankers and economists, and they were progressively reformed, especially during the period in the early 1990s when William McDonough was chairman. It was during this period that commercial bankers began to put the committee under considerable pressure, in particular through the Institute of International Finance's Working Group on Capital Adequacy, which was an association formed by large international banks. The principal outcome of this lobbying was the committee's acceptance of the internal models used by these large banks, an approach known as the internal ratings–based (IRB) approach. We start by outlining the principal elements of the two Basel Accords.

---

[1] Tarullo (2008) provides a detailed and pertinent outline of the Basel Accords.

The First Basel Accords

The first accords officially had two objectives: to assure the stability ("safety and soundness") of the international banking system, and to eliminate distortions to competition arising from the fact that some countries (Japan being the most obvious example) granted an implicit guarantee of unlimited support to their banks in the event of failure. This permitted these banks to run up massive debt at rates below those that the market would normally require, and in this way to capture significant market share in credit markets.

The principle of Basel I is remarkably simple: each bank is required to hold a minimum of total capital equal to 8 percent of its total assets, the latter being weighted by coefficients designed to reflect the credit risk of these assets.[2] The weighted sum of banking assets—risk-weighted assets—was supposed to give a measure of the total credit risk taken by the bank. The weights were themselves extremely simple: 0 percent, 25 percent, 50 percent, or 100 percent, according to the nature of the borrower or the issuer of the security (sovereign states, members and nonmembers of the Organization for Economic Cooperation and Development, commercial banks, nonbanking firms, mortgage credit, and so forth).

There is no doubt that the immediate impact of Basel I was a spectacular recapitalization of the international banking sector[3] and the reduction of distortions to competition among countries. Nonetheless, criticism was soon leveled at all sections of the accords. In particular, Basel I was accused of prompting a contraction of credit extended to individuals and firms—a credit crunch—so that banks, for instance, preferred to buy ten-year government bonds[4] rather than make loans to households and firms where the risk was weighted at 100 percent and the capital

---

[2] Given the nature of the committee, these accords had the status of recommendations applicable only to banks with a significant level of international activity. Since then, the authorities of several countries have extended the rules to all banks they regulate.

[3] See, for instance, Jackson et al. (1999).

[4] For which the capital requirement was zero, provided that the state was a member of the Organization for Economic Cooperation and Development.

requirement was consequently the full 8 percent. The problem here was that weights employed by Basel I did not correspond to the risk measures used by investors, reflected in the risk margins (or rate spreads) observed in markets (equivalent to risk premiums). Coming back to our example, sometimes the payback on ten-year government bonds was higher than that on short-term credit extended to firms with a good rating.[5] This situation arises from the fact that the default risk of a well-rated firm during a short period is very small, whereas the interest-rate risk associated with a ten-year government bond is relatively high, even if the risk of default is virtually zero. By substituting government ten-year bonds for short-term credits to corporations, banks subject to Basel I could reduce their mandated capital requirements while increasing returns on their assets. This is only a simple illustration of the many possibilities for regulatory arbitrage that Basel I opened up, which derived from the fact that the weights chosen by the committee reflected only a portion of the risks affecting banking assets (credit risk, market risk and interest-rate risk being neglected), while the weights themselves were quite imperfect (they were calculated only with regard to the institutional nature of the borrower or issuer of credit and did not truly reflect the risk of default of these institutions or the exact nature of the debt).

Faced with these criticisms, the committee immediately proceeded to amend the first Basel Accords (taking particular account of market risk and interest-rate risk) and then determined on a thorough revision, a process that in 2004 culminated in the second Basel Accords, Basel II.

The Second Basel Accords

The intrinsic motivation of Basel I was clearly identified (allowing American and British banks to compete on equal terms with Japanese banks and, more generally, preventing governments from indirectly subsidizing their banks by advancing implicit

---

[5] For this to happen, the curve of the rate had to be sufficiently steep—that is, long-term rates had to be clearly higher than short-term rates.

guarantees in the event of default), but that of Basel II is much more difficult to identify. To an outside observer the succession of reforms that created Basel II out of Basel I looks rather like a series of pragmatic contingent adjustments in which the committee sought to protect itself as far as possible from criticisms originating in the banking industry, finally ending up allowing the major international banks to determine for themselves the manner in which they would be supervised.

The starting point of the process[6] was the first consultative document (Consultation Paper 1), which was distributed in September 1998, in which the committee described the way in which it intended to measure credit risk in the future Basel II. This was once again met with a barrage of criticism (much of which came from the Institute of International Finance's Working Group on Capital Adequacy), and which for the most part repeated earlier criticisms that had questioned the competence of the Basel Committee.[7] Stung by these charges, the committee began to accept the principle of validation employed by major banks in their internal credit-risk models.

One should bear in mind that regulators are always subject to a fundamental dilemma. On the one hand, if they refuse to be influenced by the prevailing practice of the industry they regulate, they run the risk of failing to gain access to sufficient information or even being accused of incompetence. On the other hand, if they adhere too closely to these practices, they run the risk of capture by the industry they are supposed to be regulating.[8] In the case of Basel II, there is no doubt that in January 2001 (when the second consultative document was distributed), the scales tipped decisively in favor of regulatory capture.

[6] Tarullo (2008) gives a remarkable account of this.

[7] For instance, the amendment to Basel I taking account of market risk was criticized, largely for the manner in which it made use of the value at risk criterion. Alexander and Baptista (2006) suggest in particular that such usage could, paradoxically, lead to an increase in the risks taken by banks.

[8] The topic of regulatory capture was developed by economists of the Chicago School, among them George Stigler. The way these economists saw it, regulation is sometimes used by industrialists to create cartels and protect themselves from the competition of potential new entrants.

The Internal Ratings-Based Approach

The viewpoint adopted by banks, expressed more or less openly, was that the Basel Committee did not have the competence to elaborate a system of prudential regulation for credit risk and that it therefore had to draw on the models developed internally by the major international banks.

In fact, Basel II is much more complex than Basel I, notably in regard to the introduction of the "three pillars." The minimum capital ratio (the first pillar) is complemented by a much more important role for the supervisor (the second pillar), and the requirement for transparency is much more rigorous (third pillar), facilitating the exercise of a degree of market discipline as a complement to regulatory discipline. But it is the first pillar that embodies the essentials of the changes introduced by Basel II. The calculation of capital requirements is henceforth obtained from the sum of the three terms, linked respectively to credit risk, market risk, and operational risk. The general methodology used is that of value at risk (VaR),[9] generally estimated on the basis of historical data. In other words, the regulator seeks to estimate, for each risk, the amount of capital that will enable the bank to cover its losses over a determinate period (one year for credit risk), with a particular probability (99.9 percent for credit risk), assuming that future conditions turn out to be similar to past conditions (the assumption that the environment is stationary). This is very much a static "engineer's" approach to the risk of bank default, analogous to the way civil engineers calculate how much concrete has to be used in the construction of a bridge so that its probability of collapse becomes sufficiently small. This approach fails to account for the dynamic aspects of a banking institution, which is constantly seeking to renew investments and refinancing arrangements.[10] Furthermore, it fails to take into account the fact that financial risks are not exogenous but arise

---

[9] VaR represents the potential loss of an investor in respect of a portfolio of assets that can be exceeded only with some given probability (typically 0.1 or 0.5 percent) over some given time interval (ranging from one week to one year).

[10] As will be shown later, the semicollapse of Northern Rock was not brought about mainly by its inadequate capital, but more importantly by the drying up of credit for short-term refinancing.

from the behavior of economic agents. Consequently, the statistical distribution of banking and financial returns is not stationary but depends critically on the economic and regulatory environment, as well as on the individual incentives[11] confronting the many economic agents who participate in different aspects of financial intermediation.

It can be said that the principal innovation in Basel II was the validation, in measuring credit risk, of the internal ratings–based approach, which draws on a theoretical model called the asymptotic single-risk factor (ASRF). As an alternative to the standard approach, in which the regulator directly imposes weights intended to measure credit risk of a bank's various assets (a refinement of the weighting employed in Basel I), the Basel Committee offered to interested banks the prospect of using their own internal models (subject to confirmation on the part of the regulator). The regulator calculated the weights on the basis of a very complex mathematical formula, which I cannot resist introducing here:

$$K = LGD \times N\left[\frac{G(PD)}{\sqrt{1-R}} + \sqrt{\frac{R}{1-R}} \times G(0.999)\right] - PD \times LGD$$

In this formula, K designates the weights that enable the capital requirement to be calculated,

$$N(x) = \frac{1}{\sqrt{2\pi}} \int_{-\infty}^{x} \exp - \frac{t^2}{2} \, dt$$

is the cumulative function of a standard normal distribution, LGD is the loss in the event of default, $G(u) = N^{-1}(u)$ is the quantile function of the normal distribution, R is the correlation between the portfolio of loans and the macroeconomic risk factor, and PD is the probability of default.[12]

---

[11] See Ashcraft and Schuermann (2008) for a detailed diagnosis of the incentive problems arising at every level of the securitization process.

[12] This formula comes from a very elegant model, elaborated by Gordy (2003), which allows the VaR to be assessed for a diversified portfolio of credits correlated to a unique macroeconomic factor. Obviously, the price paid for the elegance

The internal models used by banks are then employed to flesh out this regulatory formula and to estimate the probability of default in the case of "IRB Foundation" (the regulator estimating the other parameters), or the set of parameters PD, LGD, and R in the event of "IRB Advanced."

A comprehensive elaboration of this formula, conjugated for various categories of borrower (sovereign governments, banks, firms) and corrected through consideration of many other factors (effective maturity, small and medium-sized firms), highlights our main criticisms. The above regulatory formula is far too complex to permit anyone external to the relationship between bank and supervisor to judge whether the supervisor has done its work properly. It is a complex function of many parameters that are practically impossible to estimate independently. Consequently, it lends the regulator a great deal of discretion in the more or less strict application of prudential criteria. One of the initial objectives of the Basel process—to suppress distortions to competition among banks in different countries by constraining the discretion of national supervisors—becomes therefore unrealizable.

At the same time, complicated as it already is, the Basel II regulatory regime is far too rough to facilitate an accurate assessment of the risk that a particular bank will fail. The management of risk within a large financial institution in fact involves an extremely complex set of methods that are more or less formalizable (stress-testing, scenario analysis, risk mapping) and that allow the board of these major institutions to take calculated risks in the interest of their shareholders. Modern risk management is more an art than a science: a very sophisticated mathematical model that captures only particular risks will always be less useful than a collection of pragmatic methods that take account of the total exposure of the institution to risk. In the case of Northern Rock, for instance, it would have been much better to direct attention

---

of this formula is that it is based on a number of totally unrealistic assumptions, such as a normal distribution especially inappropriate to the risk of default and a single unique factor for macroeconomic risk. A multifactor model with thick-tailed distributions would be infinitely more constructive but would require a statistical treatment that would be impossible to validate at the regulatory level.

to liquidity risk than seek a precise assessment of the credit risk modeled by the ASRF.

Basically, the fundamental error made by the Basel Committee derived from two deep-seated confusions:

- First, there was confusion over the objectives of prudential regulation and banking supervision. Although the managers of major banks have, like the managers of all other companies, a duty to take calculated risks for the purpose of maximizing the wealth of their shareholders, the duty of banking supervisors is very different. Their main task is to detect (as far as possible) "deviant" institutions that jeopardize the wealth of their depositors or the stability of the financial system, and impose corrective measures on them. Above all, there is no reason for banking supervisors to get involved in the everyday management of sound institutions. By contrast, it is imperative that these same supervisors take coercive action as soon as they spot dubious behavior in a distressed institution. The role of prudential ratios has then to be fundamentally revised: it is not a question of proposing, or imposing, a particular way of managing banking risk, something the regulator is in no position to do. Instead, the regulator's task is to provide simple indicators (in effect, an early warning system) that allow the conditions under which the regulator will intervene in the management of a distressed institution to be specified. As will be shown later, this philosophy inspired the notion of prompt corrective action defined by U.S. regulators in the Federal Deposit Insurance Improvement Act of 1991.
- The second confusion of the Basel Committee relates to the status of mathematical models in finance and economics. Contrary to those used in the physical sciences, the models employed in finance are only weakly predictive, and only in the short term. They are there only to clarify our qualitative understanding of extremely complex phenomena occurring in the ebb and flow of markets. In particular, they are not robust over the long run, and are subject to frequent "regime changes" each time the economic or regulatory

environment alters, or when the expectations or behavior of economic agents change, sometimes in ways quite difficult to explain.[13]

THE BREAKDOWN OF THE BASEL PRUDENTIAL REGIME

Since the creation of the Basel Committee on Banking Supervision in 1974 the stability of the international banking system has been its prime objective. Moreover, the committee eventually spent more than fifteen years seeking to improve the prudential regime it set up in 1988, when it formulated the first Basel Accords. This prolonged effort culminated in the progressive adoption by all major countries of the Basel II Accords, made public in 2004 and intended to guarantee financial and banking stability.

So, why has there been a crisis? We can discount right away any suggestion that the problem originated with institutions that were not subject to Basel II. Even though it is true that some countries (among them the United States) had not implemented Basel II when the crisis started and that U.S. investment banks were in any event entirely outside the Basel regime[14] (since they did not finance their activity by taking deposits from the public), it cannot be denied that the crisis has affected all major international banks, and these banks had mostly anticipated the principles of Basel II. Moreover, it should be remembered (1) that these major international banks had obtained from the committee a guarantee that the application of Basel II would not involve an increase of average capital requirements for all banks, and (2) that these major banks in some case benefited from a reduction of these requirements as an incentive to adopt the IRB method. This is clearly established by Blundell-Wignall and Atkinson (2008), who estimate that a reduction of £220 billion in regu-

---

[13] This is reminiscent of the way Merton Miller described the Long-Term Capital Management debacle: "In a strict sense, there wasn't any risk—if the world had behaved as it did in the past" (cited in Lowenstein 2000).

[14] In fact, these banks had accepted adherence to prudential control by the Securities and Exchange Commission, but this control seems to have been sketchy, and in any case the banks concerned have disappeared, voluntarily converted themselves into traditional bank holding companies, or been bought out since the beginning of the crisis.

lated capital for all American commercial banks was achieved in the transition to the advanced IRB system.

Why then was it necessary massively to recapitalize the international banking system when, according to the principles of the Basel prudential regulatory regime, most major banks had levels of equity capital generally considered adequate? This is the subject of the second part of this chapter. Having illustrated our diagnosis through the example of Northern Rock we will review the main possible explanations for the breakdown of the Basel prudential regime: inability to measure the individual risk of a bank failure, inability to anticipate systemic risk, and ultimately inability to manage financial innovation. For each of these dimensions we will try to diagnose the specific inadequacies of Basel II: failure to take account of liquidity risk, failure to take account of model risk, poor choice of regulatory criteria, and failure to take account of the opacity of some financial instruments. Then we will quickly review the other leading criticisms made of Basel II: procyclicality and a lack of balance between different elements (the famous "three regulatory pillars").

The Northern Rock Case

The case of Northern Rock is particularly instructive. The CEO of Northern Rock, under questioning by a Treasury committee of inquiry investigating the causes of the first run on a British bank since 1872,[15] was asked about the handsome dividend distributed to shareholders shortly before the events that led to the rescue of the bank by the British authorities. He explained with some irony that the level of equity was more than enough according to Basel II, and that he therefore considered that his shareholders had a right to benefit from his "shrewd" management of the bank.[16] In retrospect, of course, Northern Rock's business

---

[15] It is usually stated that the last previous run on a U.K. bank was on Overend Gurney (in 1866), but there was a less well-known run on the City of Glasgow Bank in 1872. I thank Charles Goodhart for this precision.

[16] Blundell-Wignall and Atkinson (2008) quote this exchange:

Mr. Fallon: "Mr. Applegarth, why was it decided a month after the first profit warning, as late as the end of July, to increase the dividend at the expense of the balance sheet?"

model, which involved financing investments in opaque and illiquid structured products through uninsured very short-term deposits, could not have been more risky. Blundell-Wignall and Atkinson (2008) provide interesting details on this case. In June 2007 the British supervisory agency, the Financial Services Authority, approved the advanced IRB approach employed by Northern Rock. But the leverage was phenomenal: £2.2 billion in equity capital for a balance sheet total of £113.4 billion. Leverage of this scale was possible because of the extremely favorable weighting of risk: less than £19 billion of risk-weighted assets (compared to £34 billion under Basel I), giving regulated capital of only 19 × 8% = £1.52 billion. By comparison, when Northern Rock's depositors panicked, the British authorities had to inject £23 billion into the bank.

Even if it had been cushioned by a larger sum of equity capital, this extreme position would have placed Northern Rock in a very precarious position. The banking supervisors found nothing to comment on, however. Basel II clearly was unable to control the risk of an individual bank failure.

Inability to Control the Risk of an Individual Bank Failure

Justifications of prudential banking regulation are of two orders: the protection of small depositors against the risk of their bank collapsing (what is called microprudential regulation),[17] and the protection of the banking system as a whole against the risk of a generalized crisis (macroprudential regulation). It turns out that, in spite of the growing recognition of systemic risk (see, for instance, Borio 2003, Rochet 2004), the Basel prudential regime remains very much centered on microprudential concerns: how

---

Mr. Applegarth: "Because we had just completed our Basel II two and a half year process and under that, and in consultation with the FSA [Financial Services Authority], it meant we had surplus capital and therefore that could be repatriated to shareholders through increasing the dividend."

Northern Rock had also been awarded the prestigious "Financial Institution Group Borrower of the Year 2006" presented by the *International Financing Review*.

[17] See Rochet (2008b, 3–4).

can the probability of the collapse of each bank be limited to what is considered an acceptable level? Later we will show the dangers of confining oneself to this individual approach. In this section, we will suggest that the Basel prudential regime is for the most part ill suited to controlling the risk of an individual bank's collapse.

This derives largely from a confusion of means and ends by the Basel Committee. Harshly criticized for the summary fashion in which credit risk was taken into account in Basel I (involving regulatory arbitrage, where banks were permitted to exploit the differences between risk measures used by regulators and by markets), the Basel Committee sought in Basel II to adopt the methods used by major banks themselves in measuring credit risk. As has been seen, the IRB method calculates capital requirements (in terms of credit risk) through an extremely complex formula involving many parameters that are difficult to measure. The regulator uses this formula to calculate capital requirements on the basis of parameters partly supplied (in the basic IRB approach) or entirely supplied (in the advanced IRB approach) by the bank's internal models.

As we have already suggested, no matter how complicated this formula may be, it captures credit risk only very imperfectly, completely neglecting the risk of illiquidity, which turned out to be critical in the subprime crisis. Furthermore, the Basel prudential regime takes into account modeling risk only via pillar 2 (discretionary intervention on the part of the supervisor), giving the supervisor great latitude in correcting more or less seriously the imperfections of pillar 1 (ratio of minimum capital). Rather than modifying the regulatory ratio in a clear and coordinated way, this task is delegated to each supervisor, which has discretion to set the level of particular requirements. But this is quite the opposite of what should be done, namely, adopt a simple capital ratio based on parameters easy to observe or estimate, and remove all discretion from the supervisor. It is not, of course, that one suspects the supervisor of dishonesty or incompetence. On the contrary, what is at issue is the protection of the banking supervisors from political pressure and the risk that the shareholders of distressed banks will resort to the courts, giving bank regulators little incentive to impose in a timely fashion coercive measures that will limit the risk of bank failure, or at the very least the social cost of liquidation.

Another error made by the committee is a failure to recognize the endogeneity of banking and financial risks. These risks are not a priori givens, but arise from decisions made by numerous economic agents active in the banking and financial system. A basic principle of economic analysis (one particular form of which is called the "Lucas critique") concerns the need to take account of changes in the behavior of agents when their economic or regulatory environment is changed. Some even think that the greatest part of financial innovation can be explained by the desire of institutions to bypass the regulatory framework to which they are subordinated (this is called regulatory arbitrage).

For example, let us consider some of the consequences of securitization that were not foreseen by regulators. By encouraging banks to dispose of all the debts that they securitized (see Franke and Krahnen 2008), regulators intended to reduce the risk of these banks failing. But in doing so, regulators reduced the incentive for these banks to scrutinize the quality of these debts, and probably increased markedly the risk of default on securities issued as the counterpart of this debt. They therefore penalized the buyers of these securities. Of course, if the regulator adopted a strictly microprudential perspective and only concerned itself with the probability of failure of each individual bank, this incentive problem would arise in only two instances:

- If the securities were bought by other banks;
- Or if the issuing bank agreed (beyond any contractual obligation and with the sole aim of preserving its reputation) to compensate buyers in case of a problem, by, for instance, repurchasing the securities at a price above their market value.

If the issuing bank irrevocably disposes of all of its securitized credits, by contrast, a regulator adopting a strictly microprudential view is not at all concerned by the fact that the issuing bank reduces its effort to prevent defaults by borrowers, and thus in effect penalizes the purchasers of the securitized credit. But such behavior is very bad for the financial system as a whole and finally leads, as we have seen, to the complete functional breakdown of some markets. It is therefore necessary that the banking regulator take a more reasonable position, not simply confining itself to the probability of failure of each individual bank, but also paying attention to the stability of the financial system as a whole. In this case the regulator must, contrary to what it actually did, encourage the issuing bank to retain a share of the securitized portfolio (a junior tranche, for example) so that it might continue to have an incentive to pay attention to the quality of its borrowers. The explicit selection of the objective the banking regulator will pursue is clearly fundamental, and this objective cannot be reduced to considering the maximum probability of default for each bank taken in isolation.

Another illustration of the problem represented by the aim of banking regulators can be found in the adoption of the criterion of VaR, which is solely concerned with the probability of default and which takes no account of losses sustained subsequent to the moment of default. By adopting this criterion, regulators encouraged banks to focus on structurally complex financial instruments (such as collateralized debt obligations—CDOs), that shifted risk in the tail of the loss distribution. Although the VaR criterion is suited to the shareholders of a commercial bank, who are protected by limited liability, it is certainly inappropriate for public authorities, which have to compensate for losses, whatever their magnitude.

Finally, other errors made by the committee, which have been extensively covered in the press, are underestimating the complexity of structured financial products and, associated with this, passing scrutiny and assessment of these new instruments on to ratings agencies. We will deal later with the advantages of market discipline, that is, the use by banking supervisors of risk measures provided by markets, whether directly (as in ratings) or indirectly (as in default spreads, the margins between market rates for loans to a particular bank and the rate on government bonds with the same maturity date). Unfortunately, one cannot always rely on the market. Market signals can sometimes be misleading, either because there are conflicts of interest between those who provide the signals (ratings agencies) and those who use them (investors),[18] or, in the event of a systemic crisis, because market prices no longer reveal the fundamental value of securities but instead are linked entirely to the liquidity available on the market at the given instant when the securities are purchased.

Inability to Anticipate Systemic Risk

The definition of systemic risk varies from one author to another. Here I employ as broad a definition as possible: systemic risk includes all events capable of imperiling the stability of the banking and financial system. These events might be macroeconomic shocks that affect all institutions simultaneously, or situations of contagion, in which the default of one bank can spread to a significant number of other banks or even imperil an element of the banking and financial infrastructure deemed "vital," which public authorities will seek to protect whatever the circumstances. Prudential regulation must therefore explicitly anticipate the various possible outcomes related to considerations that are both systematic and macroprudential. It has to be regarded precisely as the counterparty to this state involvement, aiming to limit the probability and the cost of future state intervention in such circumstances.

This notion of systemic risk is officially a constant preoccupation of banking supervisors, but up until July 2007 this risk had never materialized, at least on the international level. Some commentators even regarded this notion as a pretext used by public authorities for the rescue of a financial institution that is actually motivated by political or other, even more dubious, considerations. After all, even though more than two-thirds of the world's countries had experienced banking crises during the final two decades of the twentieth century, the international banking and financial system had never been subjected to profound and generalized disorder of the kind unleashed by the subprime mortgage crisis. In this light, perhaps it is no surprise that the Basel system of prudential regulation was entirely bereft of concrete arrange-

---

[18] For an analysis of these conflicts of interest, see Mathis, McAndrews, and Rochet (2009).

ments directed to the prevention of such a systemic crisis. As we have seen, it was organized around the concept of value at risk, that is, the level of capital sufficient to limit the probability of collapse of an individual bank to some "acceptable" level set in advance by regulators. For example, the capital requirement related to credit at risk is supposed to cover this risk with a probability of 99.9 percent over one year, which should correspond to a frequency of failure of once every millennium. The strikingly large number of banks that have experienced serious difficulties since July 2007 clearly demonstrates that banking risk was extensively underestimated by the Basel prudential regime. That very few banks have actually collapsed since the beginning of the crisis is entirely due to the more or less unconditional support they have received from their respective governments.

There are several reasons why the Basel regulators were unable to anticipate systemic risk:

- As we have seen, most of the institutions that got into difficulty were reasonably capitalized, but exposed to an important risk of lack of liquidity. In normal times, an institution whose solvency is not doubted can easily find short-term financing. As it turns out, this is no longer the case in a systemic crisis, in which interbank and monetary markets stop working.
- A systemic crisis is by definition a rare event, and statistical models drawing on data from "normal" periods are inappropriate; for example, it is now known that correlations between the returns of financial assets increase very considerably during crisis periods.
- Similarly, the models used by regulators (among them the famous ASRF applied to credit risk) sometimes employ assumptions applicable to normal periods but inapplicable to extreme events.
- Generally, there is not sufficient data available to assess in any rigorous manner some elements of the Basel regime. For example, Rebonato (2007) criticizes the use of the 99.9 percent quantile over a year for operational risk. Even if all the data available from major banks are aggregated, one will never achieve a correct estimate of an event that is,

in theory, likely to affect each bank only once in a thousand years.

Finally, the most serious criticism that can be made of the Basel regime relating to the prevention and management of risk is that it focuses on individual banks and is not at all concerned about the stability of the financial system as a whole. As the crisis has shown, however, the majority of bank rescues funded by the public purse were rationalized a posteriori not by the wish to protect the small depositors with these banks (U.S. investment banks not having such depositors, and the deposits at commercial banks being insured),[19] but rather by the need to preserve the integrity of the financial system as a whole.

Inability to Manage Financial Innovation

To use a rather simplistic but nonetheless expressive metaphor, the recent financial crisis can be thought of as the Chernobyl of securitization. The use of a relatively new technology under poorly managed conditions led in both cases to a major catastrophe. There is a degree of similarity between the two crisis scenarios. Just as nuclear technology makes possible the production of much more electricity, using less fuel, than a conventional generating plant, the securitization of a bank's debts allows it to advance much more credit to the economy on the back of much less capital.[20] To some extent the recent crisis has its origin in the fact that the financial "engineers" in charge of placing structured financial products were, to all intents and purposes, paid in proportion to the volume of their activity, without taking any account of the risks they were creating for the wider financial system. Imagine what would happen if the engineers managing a nuclear power plant were paid exclusively in proportion to the amount of

---

[19] It could be argued that, without this rescue, the cost of deposit insurance would have been higher, but in this case rescues should have been covered by the reserves of the deposit insurance system, which are funded by deposit insurance premiums, and certainly not by the injection of public funds.

[20] Extending the analogy, it could be argued that the "quality" of the capital (the fuel) necessary for such a bank is superior to the capital of a traditional bank, and the shareholders of a bank employing securitization have to be much more vigilant than those of a traditional bank.

electricity they produced, without taking any account of the risk of a nuclear accident!

Like the production of electricity by nuclear technology (but with much more rigorous safety measures), securitization worked well for about twenty years before the subprime mortgage crisis. There can be no doubt that this was a disaster waiting to happen, given the interlocked nature of the financial system. Should securitization therefore be prohibited, in much the same way that some advocate the banning of nuclear technology? This would be a rather extreme political decision, but in any case, it is necessary to authorize banks to make use of particular techniques to transfer risk, unless one is ready to reduce significantly and permanently the supply of credit to the economy.

No matter how public authorities decide to handle securitization, the torrent of financial innovation will not dry up for long. The crisis has amply demonstrated, however, that the existing mechanism for the social and political management of financial innovation was largely ineffective. Allowing regulated financial institutions to experiment with their new techniques within the vital organs of the financial system exposed the system to the vicious circle of innovation–mania–panic–overregulation.

Other Criticisms of the Basel Regime

Two other criticisms made of Basel II before the crisis remain relevant: the procyclical character of regulation, and the lack of balance between pillar 1 and the two other pillars.

PROCYCLICAL TENDENCIES

The subprime crisis is a perfect example of the procyclicality[21] of financial systems, in other words, their propensity to amplify real shocks to the economy. Relatively moderate shocks to a particular section of the U.S. credit market in July 2007 prompted a serious loss of confidence in global financial and monetary markets, dramatically reducing the capacity of markets to supply credit to households and firms (Brunnermeier 2009). This phenomenon is not unique to the present crisis. Financial history is

[21] See Rochet (2008a) for details.

full of examples of crises like this (Kindleberger 2000), featuring a succession of periods of credit expansion fed by the exuberant optimism of investors, followed by episodes of credit contraction triggered by relatively minor negative shocks that bring about important reductions in economic activity.

The imperfections of the financial system (incomplete markets, transaction costs) generally prevent economic agents from completely insuring themselves against real shocks. Moreover, these real shocks create fluctuations in the capacity of financial intermediaries (banks and insurance companies), which in turn amplify the initial shocks. This is why banks tend to lend too much during periods of expansion and not enough during recessionary periods.

Public authorities do have some room for maneuver in seeking to reduce the amplitude of these fluctuations. Governments can contribute to the stabilization of economic activity by adopting countercyclical fiscal policies. Monetary policy can also be of help here: some central banks, such as the U.S. Federal Reserve (Fed), are mandated to pursue, besides the traditional objective of price stability, a sustainable level of employment and economic activity. Nonetheless, it is widely admitted that public authorities must also keep an eye on the stability of the financial system—this is, for example, one of the other missions of the Fed and of many other central banks. As we have seen, preservation of financial stability is one of the prime justifications of prudential regulation, for example in the setting of a solvency ratio for banks. But a ratio of this kind, if it is constraining, necessarily has procyclical effects: at the low point in the economic cycle, banks sustain losses on the credit side, which reduce their equity capital (the numerator in the solvency ratio). If they do not have equity capital in excess of the regulatory minimum, they are then obliged to reduce the volume of their advanced credit. And so Basel I was already procyclical, and was in fact accused of prompting a credit contraction as soon as it came into force in 1988.

As explained for instance by Taylor and Goodhart (2004), Basel II runs the risk of being even more procyclical, in that the weights used to calculate the weighted sum of assets (risk-weighted assets, the denominator in the solvency ratio) increase at the bottom of the cycle. As has been seen, the weights depend on various indicators such as the probability of default (PD) and the loss in the event of default (LGD), both of which increase during recessionary periods. This argument has been verified in several empirical studies. For instance, Kashyap and Stein (2003) compare three methods advanced by the Basel Committee for calculating the weights corresponding to the credit risk on a banking portfolio (Standard and Poor's ratings, Moody's KMV model of credit risk, and the internal model of a major bank) and conclude that all three methods tend to procyclicality. Even so, the time horizon selected to estimate the probability of default also plays an important role. Saurina and Trucharte (2007) show that by replacing the prevailing PD with a PD averaged over the entire cycle, procyclical effects are considerably reduced. It is easy to see both the advantages and the disadvantages of such a method—as in the calculation of provisions of risk of default, a dynamic method reduces procyclical effects, on the one hand, but also reduces the informational content of the indicators used, on the other hand.

During a normal period, the majority of banks have more capital than the regulatory minimum. This (nonsystematic) margin between "economic" capital and "regulatory" capital arises from the fact that banks are also subject to market discipline: financial analysts and ratings agencies sometimes require more capital than the regulatory minimum, especially if the bank seeks to enjoy good refinancing conditions in the markets. Moreover, it is not at all rare for those managing banks to adopt prudent policies on their own initiative, maintaining some capital as a precaution in addition to the regulatory minimum, so that they might be able to cover any losses arising from unanticipated negative shocks. In fact, the best investment opportunities sometimes arise during crises or recessions, and only those banks that have been sufficiently prudent in the management of their capital are able to benefit from these opportunities. This is the view expressed by Jaime Caruana, a former president of the Basel Committee: "When banking systems are adequately capitalized . . . and risks are correctly assessed within the appropriate time horizon, the financial system becomes more stable, less procyclical, better able to promote sustainable growth, and more resilient during periods of stress" (Caruana 2004).

As a consequence, even if the capital requirements of Basel II are undeniably procyclical, it is not certain that they will noticeably accentuate fluctuations in the volume of credit advanced by banks, since banks themselves have an interest in adjusting their economic capital to dampen fluctuations.

In any case, it seems to me that any attempt to make capital requirements countercyclical (for example, 6 percent during periods of contraction and 10 percent during expansionary phases) is very hazardous, for banking and macroeconomic cycles are not always in phase, and can be quite different from one country to another. It should be recalled that the prime objective of the Basel process was initially the prevention of competitive distortions between countries that could be attributed to the discretionary support some banks received from their governments. Permitting the authorities of each individual country to reduce capital requirements at their own discretion would amount to abolishing all the efforts to harmonize prudential standards made by the Basel Committee over the past twenty years.

DISEQUILIBRIUM BETWEEN THE FIRST PILLAR AND THE OTHER PILLARS

There is a striking contrast between the sophistication and precision of pillar 1, dealing with capital ratios, and the arty haziness with which the Basel Committee presents pillar 2 (supervision) and pillar 3 (market discipline). To illustrate, the third consultation paper on Basel II devotes 132 pages to refinements of the capital ratio, as against only 16 pages to pillar 2 and 15 to pillar 3. If one wishes to set up a balanced prudential regime, this is not the way to go about it. In reality, the only concrete provisions adopted by the Basel Committee in the domains of supervision and market discipline are nothing short of disastrous. The first mistake was to leave so much discretion to national supervisors in their (more or less strict) interpretation of capital requirements in pillar 1. The implicit objective was probably to allow national supervisors latitude for correcting imperfections in the capital ratio. But if this were the case, why spend so much time specifying this ratio in such minute detail?[22] And above all, al-

---

[22] Blundell-Wignall and Atkinson (2008) quote Sheila Bair, the president of the Federal Deposit Insurance Corporation: "If the capital standards are unreli-

ways in relation to the initial aim of the Basel process—to eliminate distortions to competition and create a level playing field—is it reasonable to assume that all national administrators will be able to resist political pressure and act both promptly and decisively as soon as one of the banks in their care runs into difficulties?

In the same way, the use of market discipline (pillar 3) is a priori a good idea, but certainly not as a *substitute* for regulatory discipline. By giving private ratings agencies quasi-regulatory powers, the Basel Committee immeasurably augmented the power of these agencies and exacerbated the conflict of interest that arises from the fact that these agencies are paid by the issuers of structured securities, with the now familiar disastrous outcome. In reality, market discipline has to function as a *complement* to regulatory discipline, by providing signals that are clear and hard to manipulate, enabling the supervisor to intervene when it must while being shielded from political pressure and shareholder lawsuits. To be specific, if for example the prudential regime stipulates irrevocably that a bank has to be closed down if its capital falls below 2 percent of its weighted assets (calculated according to a simple formula capable of being externally verified), then the supervisor is obliged to act. It is then completely protected from political pressure or threats of shareholder lawsuits. If, on the other hand, he possesses (as is the case today) a great deal of discretion in making decisions, and if the regulatory formulae are so complex that they can be easily manipulated by the bank and/or the supervisor, then all kinds of opportunistic behavior are imaginable.

It must be said that, more or less by definition, market discipline does not work, or does not work very well, during financial crises. To return to the Northern Rock case, the business model that the managers chose placed them under an extreme version of market discipline: at the first whiff of suspicion about the quality of its assets, Northern Rock's refinancing operations, reliant as they almost entirely were on short-term markets, would have condemned the bank to close if the public authorities had

---

able, how can we have confidence that supervisory add-ons will be sufficient or consistent?"

not believed that intervention was necessary. This demonstrates that market discipline can function only if two conditions are guaranteed in advance:

- the government has found a way of committing itself not to intervene; and
- markets function properly, a condition that excludes periods of crisis.

It is therefore vital to foresee two distinct regimes: on the one hand, a mechanism that prevents the injection of public funds into the banking system during "normal" periods during which market discipline works; and, on the other hand, a regime explicitly built for systemic crises, during which the supervisor is not able to rely on market indicators and when the injection of public funds is sometimes indispensable.

The Necessary Reforms

Three types of reforms are necessary: (1) a much more powerful and independent banking supervisor, (2) much simpler, and easier to apply, prudential regulation, and (3) the installation of a prompt corrective action regime for the management of crises, including a special resolution regime for systematically important financial institutions.

A Powerful and Independent Banking Supervisor

A bit of political economy is needed to understand banking crises. The subprime crisis was not just a chance event. Many of its formative elements, notably the lax monetary policy of the Fed under Alan Greenspan, the granting of mortgages to borrowers hitherto considered insolvent, the placing on the market of excessive amounts of AAA-rated securities with very good returns—all of this met the demands of powerful interests. In the United States, these conditions created an environment in which the business sector collected a great deal of money and politicians gained the support of much of the electorate, and in the rest of the world fund managers were delighted to seem so talented in the eyes of their clients, capable of finding apparently nonrisky placements that also offered high returns. In a context in which such major interests meshed so closely, the occasional Cassandras who tried to sound the alarm found their voices quickly stifled.

In reality, the crisis arose from the incapacity of governments to state in a credible way that they would not act to save a failing bank, since it was only a position of this kind, firmly adhered to, that would give banks an incentive to reduce their risks during the good times.

Banks, or in any case some of them, are an essential cog in the economic machine and it is always better to keep them working rather than shut them down. There is, therefore, even in an uncorrupted democratic state, always political pressure to recapitalize them if they get into difficulty. But this solution, reasonable at the moment for each individual case, has quite disastrous long-term consequences, since it encourages bankers to take excessive risks with their clients' money. The problem arises precisely from the difficulty that governments have in making credible pronouncements about their future actions and also, of course, about the future actions of their successors.

This frailty of the modern state (inability to commit to future actions, what economists call a time-inconsistency problem) explains why central banks have been given operational independence in many countries, so that they can pursue monetary policy without fear of political pressure. Quite simply, I propose that the same independence be given to the authority supervising the banks.

The only way of breaking the vicious circle of recurrent banking crises, fed by phases of speculative mania, is to give the agencies in charge of banking supervision the power to take charge of troubled banks *before* they really endanger the funds of their small depositors and/or the stability of the financial system.

A law governing failures specific to banking institutions must be drafted, banks shareholders must be open to expropriation, and managers must be dismissed *before* the bank technically enters a condition of default. Simultaneously, the supervisory agency should have complete independence with respect to public powers and economic interest groups.[23] This must of course be accompanied by strict accountability and a posteriori responsibility of the supervisors to the legislative branch of government.

Such a reform has little chance of being adopted in a "normal" period, when business circles will oppose it. In any case, the debate is too technical to engage the public and the world of politics. By contrast, in time of crisis the public becomes very aware of the problem and the legislature has a window of opportunity. The recent crisis therefore provides us with an exceptional opportunity to set up new institutions better able to supervise and regulate banks.[24]

This is exactly what happened in Brazil, where public opinion eventually lost patience with a series of banking and financial scandals that had been very costly for the taxpayer. The Brazilian Constitution has since 1998 prohibited the use of public funds to rescue banks, as well as loans from the Central Bank to the Treasury and to nonfinancial institutions.[25]

With Brazilian arrangements in mind, I propose that the new arrangements for banking supervision be articulated around three fundamental principles:

1. Absolute prohibition against the injection of public funds into the banking sector during "normal" periods;
2. The obligation of the agency for banking supervision to intervene coercively in the management of distressed banks, in a graduated manner related to the degree of difficulty in which the bank finds itself, and in the spirit of the American Prompt Corrective Action measures incorporated in the Federal Deposit Insurance Corporation Improvement Act.[26]

---

[23] So that the number of independent agencies is not further increased, I am in favor of the central bank itself having charge of bank regulation and supervision, as it does in many countries. In this case it is important to guarantee the independence of the monetary and the prudential branches from each other during "normal" periods, whereas during crisis periods, by contrast, these branches should work as closely as possible together.

[24] As I proofread this manuscript (November 2009), it seems that public authorities all over the world have already missed this opportunity.

[25] These arrangements have since been revised and are now part of the Law on Fiscal Responsibility.

[26] It might appear surprising to give an example from the U.S. system of supervision, when this system is commonly supposed to be one of the prime instigators

The ultimate sanction, in the most extreme cases, would be the expropriation of shareholders and the dismissal of both board and management.

3. The formulation by the regulator of simple and observable criteria that would define the conditions under which the supervisor should intervene. These criteria have to be simple enough to be assessed externally, and subsequently verified by a parliamentary control commission.

Reform of Prudential Regulation

The role assigned to prudential policy must be reinterpreted: it must no longer be a matter of explaining to banks how they should manage their risks, but instead of laying down simple and verifiable criteria triggering the intervention of the supervisor.

A first corollary of such a reformulation of microprudential objectives is that solvency ratios, and more generally regulatory indicators, need to be simplified. One mathematical formula, or even several, will never entirely capture the complexity of risk management in a major banking institution; instead, what one needs is a battery of simple and easily verifiable indicators that will point up those institutions that may present problems.

As we have seen, the main causes for the failure of Basel II lay in the belief that by limiting the risk of failure for each individual bank, the stability of the entire banking and financial system might be guaranteed. The regulatory framework established to this end in fact encouraged banks to behave like sheep, all adopting similar strategies, with disastrous consequences. A situation in which 1 percent of banks collapses each year is perhaps manageable, but certainly not a situation in which there is a 1 percent probability that all banks will collapse simultaneously.

To ensure that these circumstances are not repeated, regulation has to cease creating an incentive for banks to adopt sheeplike

---

of the crisis. But in fact it seems that the gradualist approach to intervention established in the Federal Deposit Insurance Corporation Improvement Act of 1991 was never properly applied, and especially that the risk indicators used (financial leverage) were very imperfect. In any case, it should be remembered that U.S. investment banks, which played a critical role in the crisis, were not subject to supervision by the Federal Deposit Insurance Corporation.

behavior; supervisors must establish instruments that can measure the exposure of banks to macroeconomic risk.

Furthermore, it is vital to develop a measure of the risks that major banks themselves pose to the components of financial infrastructure that are deemed vital (high-value payment systems, clearinghouses for derivatives, some financial markets). At present, these vital components of financial infrastructure are often capable of covering the risk of default of individual institutions. But in general there is no coverage for multiple simultaneous failures, nor any means of preventing the propagation of default from one component of the financial infrastructure to another.

Generally, we need to think of instruments to prevent systemic risk as means for preserving the network of interactions among all financial institutions, which raises the key question: What is the boundary of this network? Should, for instance, hedge funds be subject to regulation and supervision? It is of course impossible to prevent private economic agents in the Cayman Islands from signing crazy contracts transferring risk, but one should try to protect what is considered to be vital financial infrastructure from the negative consequences of economic agents' actions.

It all comes back to the fundamental paradox of banking activity: banks are private institutions that collectively manage a fundamental public good, the financial infrastructure thought to be of vital concern. It should therefore be remembered that the grant of a banking license by a supervisor is a privilege that has to be accompanied by well-specified obligations (one could, for instance, imagine the banning of financial experiments thought liable to place the infrastructure in danger), and that this license can be revoked if necessary.

Establishment in Advance of a Credible Mechanism for Crisis Management

Two conditions are crucial for the effective functioning of supervisory systems during "quiet periods": the inability of the government to inject public funds into the banking system (to allow market discipline to work); and the use by regulators of market signals that are both simple and objective (of a kind obliging the supervisor to act as soon as a bank gets into difficulty, and to protect the supervisor from political pressure and from legal action on the part of shareholders).

As we have seen, these conditions do not hold during crisis periods. Sometimes during periods of crisis the injection of public funds is unavoidable, and it is obvious that financial markets no longer function efficiently in such periods. Consequently there is a need to define a regime specific to banking crises, analogous to emergency measures authorized for use following natural catastrophes, and for which the rules of intervention of supervisors and public authorities are distinct from those prevailing in a "normal" period.

This is a very preliminary approach to the problem and it would not be appropriate to detail the organization of a regime to be established during periods of banking crisis; instead, some suggestions have been made that can be followed up with further discussion. We will also ignore the international aspects of crisis management, which raise very sensitive issues meriting separate treatment.

If the risk of opportunistic abuse is to be avoided, notification of a "banking crisis" could be decided on only by unanimous agreement of a tripartite committee made up of representatives of the central bank (as the monetary authority), the banking supervisor (which could be a section of the central bank), and the Treasury. This tripartite committee will also take immediate charge of the tools used in the management of the crisis: placing exceptional (short- and medium-term) credit facilities at the disposal of the central bank and commercial banks, using public funds to recapitalize the banking sector in part or as a whole, and, if needed, setting up defeasance structures to deal with banks' toxic assets.

The critical issue is the definition of a rule for the sharing of the costs of intervention among the central bank, the deposit insurance fund (if it is managed autonomously, which seems crucial), and the Treasury. To avoid competitive distortion among banks, participation in the deposit insurance fund will have to be financed a priori through insurance premiums against systemic risk, paid for by financial institutions. In the same way, before protecting the equity capital of the central bank, its lending to distressed institutions will have to be made senior and collateralized.

To conclude, in banking crises as in any other kind of crisis, it is better to have defined in advance the action to be taken and who is responsible for what than to decide these matters at the last moment, under the pressure of circumstances.

CHAPTER 4

The Treatment of Distressed Banks

Mathias Dewatripont and Jean-Charles Rochet

THE RECENT FINANCIAL crisis has been multidimensional, and it has already prompted a number of analyses and policy-oriented documents.[1] This book is academic in nature, and therefore tends to emphasize principles rather than details of practical implementation. Moreover, our focus in this chapter is on the treatment of distressed banks—a key element of the regulatory architecture that has so far attracted little attention. The treatment of distressed banks cannot be dealt with in isolation from other dimensions of this architecture, however. Hence some of our recommendations will indirectly address the contextual aspect.

This chapter is concerned with potential measures G20 countries can take to deal with the international financial regime. More precisely, as far as the treatment of distressed banks is concerned, we can think of G20 actions as pursuing two possible objectives:

1. The harmonization of the treatment of distressed banks across countries in order to level the playing field while also promoting global financial stability; it is useful in this regard to distinguish individual bank distress from systemic distress.
2. The promotion of cooperation between countries in the treatment of cross-border distressed banks.

We discuss these issues in turn. A key idea underlying the analysis is that the current regulatory system is fragile and this fragility arises from the lack of any explicit attempt to harmonize the

---

[1] See, for example, Acharya and Richardson (2009), Brunnermeier et al. (2009), chapter 2 in this volume, and the Group of Thirty Report (2009) for excellent wide-ranging analyses.

treatment of distressed banks. This contrasts with the significant efforts made to harmonize capital ratios under Basel I and II. Of course, the resulting principles of harmonization were also significantly flawed, and these flaws likewise have to be addressed. But the idea that we need harmonized capital ratios is a sound one, an idea that should be extended to the treatment of distressed banks. This is very important from the perspective of politics and economic policy: whether in good or bad times, supervisors always face pressure from lobbies and from politicians that can undermine the proper functioning and stability of the financial system. There is therefore a cost in leaving important matters inadequately specified, or even entirely unspecified, and consequently left to the discretion of national supervisors. These supervisors need the ex ante protection of a system of transparent rules. Of course, such rules always incur a potential cost in terms of loss of flexibility. The current system has clearly erred in the other direction, however. We offer here a number of recommendations aimed at moving closer to a rules-based system that preserves a sufficient degree of flexibility.

Our set of recommendations is as follows. First, in dealing with *individual banks*:

- A harmonized special bankruptcy regime should be established for individual banks that involves "prompt corrective action," providing the supervisory agency with powers to limit the freedom of bank managers (possibly removing them) and shareholders (possibly expropriating them) *before* the bank is technically insolvent.
- Supervisors should have the independence, resources, and expertise necessary for the effective fulfillment of their task. If public authorities are unwilling to increase spending on supervision then, other things being equal, the regulatory regime should be simplified. Basel II did go in the wrong direction here, with big banks being allowed to compute risks themselves by using complex internal models, creating a clear conflict of interest that hampered proper oversight by supervisors.
- In terms of the structure of regulation, one should not allow banks to play off one regulator against another (as has

been the case in the United States with the Office of the Comptroller of the Currency and the Office of Thrift Supervision). Beyond this, although consolidated supervision—bundling ex ante monitoring and ex post intervention—allows for cost savings and simpler coordination, it may reduce accountability. Such reduction in accountability can be avoided by reducing regulators' discretion in the decision to intervene (as in the U.S. Federal Deposit Insurance Corporation Improvement Act).

- The signals triggering intervention should be regarded only as crude indicators of the risk of potential problems. Simplicity is therefore crucial, since it reduces scope for manipulation and enhances transparency and credibility.
- A single capital requirement, even when it is very complex, is not enough to limit risk taking by banks. Therefore regulators need to design a battery of indicators to provide both simple signals of the various dimensions of banking risk (including liquidity and transformation risks, risks of large losses, exposure to macroeconomic shocks), and also standards against which decisions can be made regarding the need for supervisory corrective action.
- Other dimensions of regulatory control capable of curbing any incentive for excessive risk taking on the part of managers of banks must be explored: the remuneration of senior managers, shareholder representation, and internal risk management systems. This cannot remain as vaguely defined as it is in pillar 2 of Basel II.

Second, regarding *banking crises*:

- Public authorities should expect crises to happen. They should establish a mechanism permitting a crisis to be formally declared (an event that will allow the release of public funds). This means formalizing ex ante cooperation between the relevant actors (central bank, supervisor, treasury) with this contingency in mind.
- Ex post crisis management should be mindful that undercapitalized banks do not function well. "Real" recapitalization should be the aim, even if costly. Several options are open—temporary nationalization, insuring bank loans, or

parking toxic assets in bad banks. The objective should be to restart lending by properly capitalized banks without delay, and without an excessive burden on taxpayers.

• Under the current regulatory regime, the maintenance of adequate capitalization in bad times has procyclical effects. This can be overcome by introducing automatic stabilizers into the regulatory system, such as higher capital ratios in good times, dynamic provisioning, capital insurance (privately or publicly provided), or procyclical deposit insurance premiums.

Finally, regarding *international cooperation* in crisis management:

• In economic areas that are supposedly highly integrated, like the European Union, there should be a move toward a centralized supervisor and centralized deposit insurance.
• If the integration of the world banking market is to be sustained, serious consideration should be given to the partial centralization of supervision and deposit insurance at the world level.
• In the absence of such centralization, it is important to foster best practices by establishing credible memorandums of understanding for cross-border banking crisis management between authorities, detailing in particular the respective rights and obligations related to intervention thresholds and deposit insurance.

REFORMING PRUDENTIAL POLICY FOR DISTRESSED BANKS

The regulatory/supervisory systems of most G20 countries have been strongly influenced by the Basel process, initiated in the 1980s by the Basel Committee on Banking Supervision. The aims of this process were essentially two: promoting the safety and soundness of the international banking system, and guaranteeing a level playing field by eliminating competitive distortions arising from the implicit support provided by some governments to their domestic banks.

Although the Basel process has clearly contributed to the harmonization both of risk management practices by banks and regulatory requirements across countries,[2] and was still being reformed (Basel II) when the crisis hit, the regime was incapable of containing the crisis. We suggest that Basel II should be thoroughly reformed, and that the objectives of regulatory/supervisory systems should be systematically reassessed.

Implementing a Special Bankruptcy Regime for Banks

Several events during the present crisis have revealed that the banking authorities of several G20 countries did not possess legal powers sufficient to treat banking distress in a timely and efficient way. Moreover, the discretion given to domestic supervisors by Basel II's pillar 2 turned out to be counterproductive in the management of the crisis, since it exposed them to political pressure and threats of lawsuits by the shareholders of distressed banks. Generally speaking, it is not a good idea to harmonize regulatory requirements for banks if enforcement of these requirements is left to the discretion of domestic supervisors who operate under political and legal constraints that differ a great deal from country to country.

Thus the first priority for creating a level playing field for international banking, avoiding a race to the bottom with regard to the enforcement of prudential policy, is the reform and harmonization of the law of bankruptcy for banks. Banks are not ordinary firms: partly because of the existence of deposit insurance, their shareholders and managers have considerable scope in "gambling for resurrection" even when facing extreme solvency problems.[3] In the absence of timely supervisory action, shareholders and managers still have an interest in continuing the bank's activity, despite this increasing the ultimate damage to the deposit insurance fund and to the financial system as a whole.

---

[2] The Basel Accords were initially designed for internationally active banks, but they have been adopted, after some modifications, by the domestic regulators of many countries.

[3] This has been well documented in the case of the U.S. savings and loan crisis of the 1980s; see, for example, Dewatripont and Tirole (1994) for an overview.

As Goodhart (2008, 353) elegantly states:

A key feature of any bank insolvency regime must involve some expropriation of shareholder rights, and, whatever the compensation arrangement for shareholders it is bound to generate . . . a claim that they were robbed of their property. . . . So the key for closure, and the treatment of shareholders, is a central issue.

A good point from which to begin the harmonization of bank insolvency procedures would be the U.S. system created in 1991 under the Federal Deposit Insurance Corporation Improvement Act, centered on the important notion of prompt corrective action.[4] This system has the advantage of initiating crisis-related action gradually, classifying banks into five categories by capital ratio: well capitalized (capital ratio >10%); adequately capitalized (>8%); undercapitalized (<8%); significantly undercapitalized (<6%); and critically undercapitalized (<2%). The first two categories face no restrictions, but the bottom three categories face increasingly severe restrictions on action (dividend payments, asset growth, acquisitions, and, in the extreme, receivership). The key idea is to allow the supervisor to intervene before things get out of hand.

There is broad agreement that prompt corrective action has had a beneficial effect,[5] and there are also theoretical analyses in its favor (Freixas and Parigi 2008).

Our first recommendation, therefore, is:

- A harmonized special bankruptcy regime should be established for banks involving prompt corrective action, lending the supervisory agency powers to limit the freedom of the bank's senior managers (possibly removing them) and of shareholders (possibly expropriating them) *before* the bank is technically insolvent.

---

[4] Brazil introduced a similar system, which would be worth examining.
[5] See, for example, Benston and Kaufman (1997), and Aggarwal and Jacques (2001).

Establishing Strong and Independent Supervisory Agencies

A necessary complement to the reform of the bankruptcy law for banks is the protection of supervisors from pressure by politicians and lobbyists.

This is only possible with a strong, independent, well-staffed, and well-paid supervisor. And it is likely to be easier with consolidated supervision of all government-insured deposit-taking institutions in each country. The American situation is clearly undesirable: there, the ability of financial institutions to choose between two ex ante supervisors—the Office of the Comptroller of the Currency (OCC) for banks and the Office of Thrift Supervision (OTS) for savings and loans—has led (see box A) to underregulation by the OTS, mainly because its budget depends on the number and size of the institutions under its supervision.

Consolidated supervision can in some cases have drawbacks, however, even if it allows administrative cost savings. Since early detection of bank distress is not always possible, supervisors may be tempted to hide a bank's problems in the hope that they might disappear and therefore never reveal their own failure to have identified these problems sufficiently early.[6] This creates a potential conflict of interest between ex ante supervision and ex post intervention. In this respect the American system has its advantages, with its distinction between the institution in charge of ex ante supervision (the OCC for banks and the OTS for savings and loans) and the institution in charge of dealing with distressed banks ex post, the Federal Deposit Insurance Corporation (FDIC). Moreover, providing supervisors with a clear, focused task can enhance their accountability. Indeed, as shown by evidence on the behavior of public agencies,[7] the simpler their task, the easier it is to evaluate how well they have performed, that is, to keep them accountable.

Note, however, that there are various means of addressing the issue of political pressure and accountability, by using simple, publicly observable (and thus hard to manipulate) mandatory criteria for triggering regulatory intervention. Once again, this

[6] See Dewatripont and Tirole (1994) for a discussion.
[7] See Wilson (1989); see also Dewatripont, Jewitt, and Tirole (1999) for an incentive-theoretic perspective.

Box A. Office of Thrift Supervision:
Weak Supervision in the United States

The Office of Thrift Supervision in the United States has been a comparatively weak and excessively tolerant regulator, placing emphasis on seeking further deregulation rather than monitoring the institutions under its supervision. In particular, it allowed:

1. Washington Mutual to grow fast through very aggressive "predatory lending" practices, which led the firm into bankruptcy;[8]
2. IndyMac Bank to backdate a capital injection in order to avoid sanctions and supervision;[9] and
3. Countrywide Financial to leave the banking regulator OCC to join the more permissive regulatory oversight of the OTS.[10]

is an advantage of the prompt corrective action doctrine of the FDIC.

Our recommendations for the organization of supervision are:

- Supervisors should have the independence, resources, and expertise to conduct their tasks properly. If public authorities are unwilling to raise supervisory budgets, this indicates, all things being equal, that the regulatory regime should be simplified. Basel II did move in the wrong direction here, the big banks being permitted to calculate risks through the use of their own complex internal models, a task involving a clear conflict of interest and oversight of which proved beyond the capability of the supervisors.

- Regarding the regulatory regime, banks should not be permitted to play one regulator against the other, as happened in the United States with the OCC and the OTS. Beyond this, although consolidated supervision—bundling ex ante

---

[8] See Appelbaum and Nakashima (2008a).
[9] See Appelbaum and Nakashima (2008b).
[10] See Appelbaum and Nakashima (2008a).

monitoring and ex post intervention—permits cost savings and simplifies coordination, it may reduce accountability. Reducing the discretion of national supervisors regarding the decision to intervene would go a long way to remedy this.

A Set of Simple Regulatory Requirements, Rather than a Single, Complex Capital Ratio

The Basel Committee on Banking Supervision has placed too much emphasis on its capital adequacy requirement. The Northern Rock episode, together with several others, has shown that a solvent bank can rapidly become distressed for lack of liquidity and that transformation risk cannot be neglected. In the case of Northern Rock, for example, Blundell-Wignall, Atkinson, and Lee (2008) point out that in June 2007 (roughly three months before the depositor run started) its regulatory capital requirement (computed on the basis of Basel II risk weights and approved by the Financial Services Agency) was slightly more than £1.5 billion, while British authorities had ultimately had to inject around £23 billion to bail the bank out—more than fifteen times the regulatory requirement simply to keep the bank alive.

Similarly, the idea that the capital buffer needed to cover credit risk should be computed through a complex regulatory formula using parameters taken from banks' own internal models has turned out to be a terrible idea. The internal risk-based approach to credit risk uses a regulatory formula based on a theoretical model (the asymptotic single-risk factor model). This formula is simultaneously too simple to be a good predictor of credit losses (it assumes, in particular, a unique macroeconomic risk factor and normality of loss distributions) and too complicated to be verifiable by a third party (as it requires the calibration of several parameters, such as the probability of default and the loss given default, which are very difficult to estimate).[11]

In any case, it is not the job of supervisors to decide on the level of capital held by commercial banks, nor more generally on the risk management strategies that such banks should follow.

[11] See chapter 3 for a discussion.

These are business decisions normally best left to the judgment of the managers and administrators of banks. It is only when supervisors anticipate that a bank is likely to face distress in the near future (and therefore cause problems for its depositors or for the financial system as a whole) that supervisors can and must intervene. As the recent crisis has shown, indicators for future distress cannot be condensed into one single summary capital ratio, even if it is very complex. Instead, we believe that regulatory intervention should be triggered by a number of relatively simple (and publicly verifiable) indicators, including measures of liquidity risk, exposure to macroeconomic shocks, and bilateral exposure to other banks or financial institutions.

The Basel Committee's emphasis on the probability of failure of individual banks (epitomized by the use of the value at risk criterion) was obviously misplaced. Value at risk is probably a good indicator for banks' shareholders, who have the protection of limited liability. It is also probably a good indicator for the bank managers who pay close attention to their institutions' credit ratings, computed from the estimated probability of failures. Value at risk is clearly not a good indicator for public authorities, however, since it does not take into account the upper tail of losses, which will have to be covered by depositors or, more likely, by the government.

There is another, more important, reason why the focus on the probability of failure for individual banks may have been inappropriate: the absence of systemic considerations. A 1 percent probability of failure means either that 1 percent of the banks fail every year or, alternatively, that the whole banking system fails every hundred years—quite distinct outcomes. Therefore it is crucial for regulators to find ways of discouraging herding behavior by banks, or at least penalizing excessive exposure to the business cycle. New indicators of risks must be designed based on correlation with aggregate activity rather than absolute probability of failure.

Similarly, the prime reason for public intervention on the part of central banks and treasuries during the recent crisis has been the protection of the financial system as a whole, and in particular "core infrastructures" such as high-value payment and clearing and settlement systems. Anticipating (rationally) that public authorities are bound to intervene if these infrastructures are in danger, banks have neglected risk prevention in respect of these core infrastructures. To contain moral hazard it is therefore necessary for regulators to find ways to penalize, or at least limit, the externalities that large and complex banking organizations exert on these core infrastructures. A possible alternative (or complement) would be to impose on these core infrastructures risk prevention measures that, in the event of the closure or restructuring of a large and complex banking organization (previously deemed systemic), might insulate such activities from the continued functioning of the core infrastructure. In the same vein, if central counterparties such as clearinghouses are created in order to limit aggregate risk on credit-default swaps and some over-the-counter derivatives, appropriate protection measures would have to be introduced for participants in these central counterparties.

Finally, the notion that fine-tuned capital requirements suffice to moderate the incentive for managers to take excessive risks stands revealed as grossly incorrect. Other instruments, such as some form of control over managers' remuneration, together with the implementation of appropriate internal governance measures and adequate risk-management systems, are much more suited to curb risk-taking incentives. It is more reasonable to conceive regulatory capital requirements as defining, in combination with other indicators, the thresholds for supervisory intervention, rather than seeking to impose a specific regime of risk management on banks.

Our recommendations in this section are:

- One should think of the signals triggering intervention as admittedly crude indicators of the risk of potential problems. Simplicity is therefore crucial, because it reduces the scope for manipulation and enhances transparency and credibility.
- A single capital requirement, even where it is very complex, is not enough to limit risk taking by banks. It is therefore necessary to design a battery of indicators that can provide simple signals for the various dimensions of banking risks (including liquidity and transformation risks, risks of large

losses, and exposure to macroeconomic shocks) and be simultaneously used to determine whether supervisory corrective action is needed.

- There are other dimensions of regulatory control requiring exploration that might explicitly curb the incentives for managers to take excessive risks: senior management remuneration, shareholder representation, and internal risk management systems. These ways of curbing managers' incentives to take excessive risk cannot remain as vaguely defined as in pillar 2 of Basel II (that is, its supervisory pillar).

MACROECONOMIC AND SYSTEMIC CONSIDERATIONS

Some banks achieved staggering growth rates in recent years, both nationally and internationally. This is in large part a result of regulatory changes at the national level (e.g., the elimination of restrictions on interstate banking in the United States) and also internationally (e.g., the elimination of restrictions on the activities of foreign banks in many countries, or the Single Market Program in the European Union, where a wave of mostly domestic mergers was followed by cross-border mergers). This means that the size of individual banks grew tremendously, both in large countries such as the United States and in small countries, where banks became very large indeed relative to GDP (Iceland being the most extreme case).

This development has several consequences for bank supervision. The first involves political economy considerations, such as the independence of the bank supervisor and the need for simple, objective criteria for determining when the supervisor should intervene with distressed banks, which have already been discussed. Such considerations are magnified by the "too big to fail" syndrome. Large institutions always possess significant bargaining power in normal times, expressed in their lobbying of governments and supervisors. The aftermath of the Lehman Brothers bankruptcy has, moreover, clearly indicated that one cannot afford to let big institutions fail, even if the cost of a bailout is significant and therefore politically unattractive. This unavoidably raises the bargaining power of major banks vis-à-vis supervisors in times of distress, reinforcing the need for the bank supervisors to be independent and to have a high level of expertise.

Beyond this, it is important for public authorities to face the facts: banking crises do happen in market economies. It is therefore important to have explicit crisis-management mechanisms established before crises happen. Given the tendency for markets to overreact,[12] market discipline stops working during times of systemic crisis and is replaced by destabilizing panics. When this happens the government has to step in, and quite possibly inject public funds. Three issues have to be discussed here: (1) Who decides when we are in a crisis? (2) What should be done ex post? and (3) How might the probability and social cost of a crisis be reduced?

Regarding the first question, it is important to include the three main actors in the decision process: the central bank, the supervisor, and the treasury. Each has independent access to relevant information, and the treasury brings with it democratic legitimacy. In declaring a crisis, the treasury's task would be to permit the release of public funds, which should not be allowed during normal times. In regard to the exact decision process following which a crisis can be declared, one has to keep in mind two objectives: (1) it is important to avoid excessive use of public funds through excessively frequent crisis declaration; and (2) it is also important when a "real crisis" hits that it be promptly declared, triggering the release of the necessary public funds. The successful achievement of both objectives follows only if a crisis-management system has been devised ex ante, and if regular consultation takes place among the central bank, the supervisor, and the treasury at the highest level.[13]

Regarding the second issue of ex post crisis management, the fact that undercapitalized banks do not function well as credit providers to the economy should be kept in mind. Although there

---

[12] Although somewhat extreme (as discussed, for example, in Caballero 2009), the recent crisis is a good example of the volatility of markets. It is for this reason, for example, that, in "normal times," even the firms that have access to disintermediated finance rely on banks for credit lines as insurance against the possibility of direct finance drying up.

[13] Something that seems not to happen now. See, for example, Davies (2008, 365) for the case of the United Kingdom.

is a natural tendency for public authorities to delay (fiscally costly) action in the hope that the situation will improve while they sit it out, this is typically a very bad idea. There is evidence of that in the contrast between Scandinavia and Japan in the 1990s. Rapid, real recapitalization has to be preferred to fudging accounting standards and pretending that the existing levels of capitalization are in fact quite acceptable, or permitting low capital ratios in hard times. The latter was tried in the U.S. savings and loan crisis of the 1980s and it certainly did not work.[14] It is therefore worrisome to witness the current weakening of some accounting rules in order to allow banks to "look better."

Ex post recapitalization of individual banks by public authorities in times of crisis can take several forms:[15] partial (or full) nationalization, insurance provision for bank loans, or the purchase of "toxic" assets to be parked in a "bad bank."[16] Our feeling is that there is no consensus among academics about the best way to proceed. Some principles seem obvious, however: (1) at least as far as banks that are performing worse than the average of the sector are concerned, there is clearly no reason to protect shareholders or managers in the process; the goal should be to protect depositors and taxpayers (we assume that workers have access to the same safety net as workers in nonfinancial companies); (2) although the first principle favors a cost-minimizing recapitalization, a second principle is that speed matters too—this process should not be so slow as to trigger panics or inappropriate (lack of) lending. The goal is to get healthy banks working as soon as possible.

---

[14] See, for example, Dewatripont and Tirole (1994) for an overview of this episode.

[15] We do not consider here "universal" intervention mechanisms intended to provide assistance to all banks; on this, see Caballero (2009) and Suarez (2008), among others.

[16] Interestingly, this issue generated significant research during the transition from central planning to a market economy in former communist countries in the 1990s. See, for example, Mitchell (2001), and Aghion, Bolton, and Fries (1999), who argue that a mixture of recapitalization and the liquidation of nonperforming loans can under some conditions be the optimal solution for a government trying to serve the interests of taxpayers while being at an informational disadvantage with respect to bank management concerning the quality of the loan portfolio.

Finally, what about reducing ex ante the probability and social cost of a systemic crisis? This is connected to the debate on reducing the procyclicality of regulation and has quite rightly been the subject of various analyses. Brunnermeier (2009) describes very well the negative externalities banks in trouble impose on other banks when trying to raise their capital ratios, for example by selling assets. It is indeed important for prudential regulation to take into account economywide indicators and not simply individual bank solvency.

Let us stress once again the need to avoid the danger of bank undercapitalization in bad times. Reducing procyclicality could then mean aiming at "adequate" capital ratios in bad times and higher ratios in good times, so as to limit the vicious circle discussed in Brunnermeier (2009). One avenue among others this article discusses is Spanish-style dynamic provisioning. Alternatively, to limit the overall amount of capital banks need to have (and the associated cost of holding it), one could follow the suggestion of capital insurance made by Kashyap, Rajan, and Stein (2008). Under this system, banks would pay an insurance premium to institutions against a promise of capital infusion in times of crisis.

The scheme put forward by Kashyap and his coauthors is ingenious. They are confident that private institutions or investors would be willing to provide such capital insurance, but this may be too optimistic. Such insurance could also be provided by governments, however. This is in fact what happens anyway when governments end up recapitalizing banks in times of crisis. The difference from what has happened so far is that the government could, ex ante, charge periodic insurance premiums for such "catastrophic capital insurance." Similarly, it is conceivable to require ex ante that banks having access to emergency liquidity assistance by the central banks pay a periodic fee for this service.

Procyclical capital ratios and capital insurance are two ways to introduce automatic stabilizers into the regulatory system, just as we have automatic stabilizers in fiscal policy, that is, an anticyclical deficit policy. In this case, the goal is to ensure adequately capitalized banks in times of crisis while limiting the procyclical effect of regulation. Another idea that would go in the same direction would be the introduction of procyclical deposit insurance premiums (an idea discussed by Dewatripont and Tirole 1994).

Our recommendations in this section are:

- Public authorities should expect crises to happen. They should establish a mechanism that enables a crisis to be formally declared (an event that will release public funds). Ex ante cooperation between the relevant actors (central bank, supervisor, and treasury) is required, with this contingency in mind.
- Ex post crisis management should bear in mind that undercapitalized banks do not function well. "Real" recapitalization is necessary, even if costly. There are several possible options—temporary nationalization, insuring bank loans, or parking toxic assets in bad banks. The objective should be to restart lending by properly capitalized banks with minimal delay, without excessively burdening taxpayers.
- Under the present regulatory regime, the maintenance of adequate capitalization in bad times has procyclical effects. For this to be avoided, automatic stabilizers must be introduced into the regulatory system: higher capital ratios in good times, dynamic provisioning, capital insurance (privately or publicly provided), or procyclical deposit insurance premiums.

INTERNATIONAL COOPERATION

Globalization has underlined both the current limits of international cooperation in the treatment of distressed banks and the need for improvements in such cooperation. There is a tension between the tendency to favor the growth of international banks (through global or regional pro-trade and pro–capital mobility policies) and the reliance on national (whether home- or host-country) supervisors.

We will start our discussion with the case of the European Union, where cross-border banks have been very actively encouraged. We will then take a more global view. Here we consider relationships between large economic areas with more limited cross-border banking links, but also the case of emerging economies where foreign banks have become very significant.

The Case of the European Union

In the European Union there is a significant tension between national regulators and newly created cross-border banks, encouraged by the Single-Market initiative. Two competing policy rationales have emerged in recent years. The first argument points to the potential of a single market and the productivity gains resulting from cross-border mergers. The second argument emphasizes the need for member states to retain national ownership of their big banks for reasons of strategic control or, even more simply, national pride.

The recent experience of the banking and insurance group Fortis is very instructive in this regard (see box B for details).[17] The 2007 takeover battle for ABN Amro, ultimately "won" by the trio Royal Bank of Scotland, Santander, and Fortis, was hostile and controversial; it also turned out to be much too expensive for the buyers. Nonetheless, this was very much in line with the Single-Market Program since it accelerated cross-border banking ties. Because it broke up a "Dutch jewel," however, it was also extremely unpopular in the Netherlands. The question then arose of which national regulator should be the lead supervisor of the Belgian-Dutch Fortis. This argument did not enhance cooperation between public authorities when the crisis came in September 2008, of which Dutch authorities took advantage by reasserting control over "their" share of the bank.

The lesson of this episode is that one can expect competition to generate occasional controversy, especially when things go sour ex post because of business mistakes or market reversals. Nationalistic reactions are to be expected in such circumstances, especially since national authorities take a quite different view of the acquisition of national firms by foreign ones than the acquisition of foreign firms by national ones.

---

[17] Also instructive is the case of the Icelandic banks and the relations between Iceland (a member of the European Economic Area, but not of the European Union) and U.K. authorities.

Box B. The Fortis Case: Limits to International Cooperation in Rescue Efforts

In May 2007, together with the Royal Bank of Scotland and Santander, the Belgian-Dutch banking and insurance group Fortis bought ABN Amro for a record €71 billion. This was the result of a hostile takeover battle, which the trio won against the senior management of ABN Amro supported by Barclays Bank, thanks to a bid that was higher than the equity offer of Barclays and included 80 percent cash.

This offer involved splitting ABN Amro's activities among the three banks, which "disappointed" Dutch public authorities. It is to be noted that, in terms of oversight, Belgium was and remained lead regulator of Fortis, despite the importance of the growth in Dutch activities that the acquisition of the ABN Amro business implied.

For Fortis, the deal was risky, since it meant buying for €24 billion the Dutch activities of ABN Amro together with its private banking and asset-management operations, at a time when the market capitalization of Fortis was around €40 billion. The deal, together with a €13 billion equity issue, was overwhelmingly approved by Fortis's shareholders in August 2007, however.

Difficulties surfaced in June 2008, with the announcement of a new equity issue and the cancellation of dividend payments, both in contradiction of earlier promises. This immediately led to a sharp decline in the stock price, as well as the resignation of the CEO, Jean-Paul Votron, in July 2008.

Fortis's weakness proved fatal after the Lehman Brothers failure and subsequent market meltdown. By September 24, interbank lending to Fortis had collapsed and significant deposit withdrawals were starting to take place. Since Fortis was faced with staggering liquidity needs (dozens of billions of euros by September 29), the governments of Belgium, Luxembourg, and the Netherlands agreed to a concerted recapitalization (against equity stakes) on September 28, committing, respectively, €4.7 billion, 2.9 billion, and 4 billion to Fortis Belgium, Fortis Luxembourg, and Fortis Netherlands.

This agreement failed to calm the markets, however, obliging the National Bank of Belgium to provide massive emergency liquidity assistance to Fortis over the succeeding few days. A second round of negotiations then followed, with the Dutch side on October 3 buying the Dutch activities of Fortis as well as its ABN Amro activities for a combined total of €16.8 billion. The Dutch finance minister, Wouter Bos, went on Dutch TV boasting that "they had managed to buy the better part of Fortis, leaving the worse one to the Belgians." It was revealed later that the Dutch side had never paid the €4 billion promised on September 28.

After the departure of the Dutch part of Fortis, the Belgian government decided to sell most of the remainder of Fortis activities to BNP-Paribas. Court opposition by Fortis shareholders (unhappy about the consequences of the deal on the price of Fortis Holding shares) managed to delay this operation for several months, due to the legal uncertainties of bank rescue procedures in Belgium. The sale to BNP-Paribas was in the end successful, but this saga had in the meantime led to the resignation of the Belgian prime minister.

For more details see, for example, van de Woestyne and van Caloen (2009).

As with protectionism in general, such adverse asymmetric reactions have to be kept under control through a credible set of legal provisions. The starting point of such provisions should be the fact that national supervisors can be expected to be pressured to pursue national objectives, just as public supervisors can be expected to face lobbying by national industry.

Current practice is not reassuring in this respect, however.

Indeed, reliance on national supervisors—currently, consolidated oversight by the home-country supervisor being supplemented with domestic oversight by the host-country supervisor—requires coordination and cooperation that will be tested in time of crisis, as the Fortis example demonstrates. Note that the Fortis crisis occurred just after the introduction of the European memorandum of understanding that was intended to promote cooperation in financial stability and crisis management! Although this memorandum of understanding is full of good intentions (regarding the exchange of information, the involvement of all interested parties, the pursuit of the interests of the banking group as a whole, "equity"), its problem is that it remains "a flexible tool that is, however, not enforceable," as emphasized by Praet and Nguyen (2008, 371).[18]

Although it is certainly possible to beef up such memorandums and render them more binding, one has to face the facts: If one really wants to promote the Single Market in banking (which makes sense if one wants to pursue it in nonfinancial sectors), and therefore the emergence of European and not merely national banks, it is only logical that one should also favor the emergence of a European supervisor and of a European deposit insurer. We understand that this is not an obvious goal—see Lannoo (2008), for example, on some obstacles to centralization, an objective to which the CEPS Task Force subscribes—but we think it a necessary one. In this respect, the de Larosière Report (de Larosière et al. 2009) goes in the right direction by recommending strengthened cooperation between national supervisors,[19] but it falls short of advocating the centralization of deposit insurance, probably because it internalizes the desire of national treasuries to maintain their independence.

Note that the goal we just stated is related to the Single Market, that is, it applies to the entire European Union, not just the euro zone. This does complicate matters, since there would be an asymmetry between central banks, involving several players, and an EU-wide supervisor and deposit insurer. The case for a euro-

---

[18] This view is shared by the CEPS Task Force Report; see Lannoo (2008).
[19] And the same is true for the follow-up European Regulation.

zone supervisor and deposit insurer seems therefore to be all the stronger. It is important, however, to stress the need for much more strongly coordinated enforcement mechanisms than those that currently exist wherever two territories face significant cross-border banking relationships.

Our recommendation in this section is:

- In economic areas that are supposed to be highly integrated, such as the EU, one should move toward a centralized supervisor and a centralized deposit insurer.

International Coordination in General

The European Union is, in a sense, an extreme case of economic integration. Note, however, that many emerging economies are confronted with very significant foreign bank presences. There, too, the need for coordination in times of crisis—and in particular the issue of who looks after the depositors—is crucial, especially since these emerging countries have more limited means of effectively guaranteeing deposits. A crisis in any one country where depositors were left unprotected could have devastating effects, triggering bank runs in other countries in similar circumstances.

The problem is less severe for intercontinental relations between major wealthy economies or between emerging economies because (1) they have more means at their disposal to deal with crises, or (2) they have more limited cross-banking relations, even though these have been growing over time, especially with the opening up of banking markets and the spread of risks through securitization.

Let us emphasize again that, unfortunately, the regulatory and supervisory safeguards have been increased in line with these developments. Indeed, as Asser writes:

> To protect banks and banking systems against the risk of international financial contagion, bank regulators around the world have embarked on an extensive program of harmonizing prudential banking standards among countries and fostering closer cooperation between national bank regulators. . . . It is fair to

say that, as a result, the principal licensing and prudential requirements written into national banking laws have reached a high degree of uniformity. One of the reasons for this success is that it has been comparatively easy to identify best practices for these requirements.

In contrast, little international uniformity of law or practice exists in the area of banking regulation governing the treatment of banks in distress. (Asser 2001, 3)

Although recent history has shown that the "success" of harmonized capital ratios should not be exaggerated, it is true that the treatment of banks in distress remains unharmonized. Clearly, this can lead to very many problems, especially if we bear in mind that crisis management occurs under great time pressure. Let us here draw attention to just two of these problems:

First, there is the matter of when public intervention can take place, and what the powers of public intervention might be. We emphasized earlier that the American principle of prompt corrective action is a good one; but this system is definitely not generalized, making such prompt action unavailable in other countries.

Second, and most important, is the question of depositor protection. Note that banks, when setting up operations in foreign countries, can establish subsidiaries—which then have legal standing in that country and become national firms—or simply branches, which remain an integral part of the bank. As Krimminger points out, however, even for branches, deposit insurance rarely extends beyond a country's borders:

Under most national deposit insurance systems, deposits of domestic branches are insured by the domestic deposit insurance system and deposits in a host country are insured, if at all, by the host country's deposit insurance scheme. Under US law, depositors in foreign branches of a US bank are not insured under the FDIC's deposit insurance and are subordinated to uninsured depositors of the US branches in the distribution of the proceeds from the sale of the bank's assets. Depositors in foreign branches of US banks are covered by FDIC deposit insurance only if the deposit is payable in the US in addition to the foreign branch. (Krimminger 2008, 384)

There are, therefore, clear potential incentive problems facing the home supervisor in terms of consolidated supervision, with the risk of being pressured to "limit damages" and leave part of the mess to foreign countries. This can be really dangerous in terms of contagion.

Although it is beyond the scope of this brief chapter to analyze in detail the way forward in cooperation for crisis management, we can highlight a couple of general principles:

1. Although creation of a global supervisor and deposit insurer may be unattainable, this should be considered seriously if further integration of the banking market is contemplated. What applies to the EU Single Market applies, mutatis mutandis, to a single world market. Concretely, one could give real powers to a supranational authority like the Basel Committee on Banking Supervision.

2. If one thinks that centralization is either impossible or undesirable, one should at least get serious about joint crisis management. The joint goals of avoiding contagion and avoiding regulatory arbitrage by banks should be kept in mind. We have already stressed the need to harmonize intervention thresholds, following a principle such as prompt corrective action. Moreover, if one keeps the idea of domestic deposit insurance, whatever the legal form of cross-border banking relationships, it is crucial to think of a more even-handed approach between home-country and host-country supervision. Indeed, the decision of whether to "save" a bank, and therefore fully protect all its depositors, and under what conditions, should in fact be one taken jointly by the various relevant authorities. More generally, in the absence of a supranational supervisor, what is required is an ex ante credible agreement, or memorandum of understanding, between the various countries involved concerning the manner in which supervisory and deposit-insurance responsibilities are to be shared. Such a memorandum of understanding should be as explicit as possible in order to have a chance of functioning in times of crisis. Once again, such memorandums of understanding should be standardized so that best practices are diffused.

Our recommendations in this section are:

- If one wishes to maintain the process of integrating the world banking market, one should seriously consider partial centralization of supervision and deposit insurance at the world level.
- In the absence of such centralization, it is important to foster best practices by establishing credible memorandums of understanding for cross-border banking crisis management between authorities that detail, in particular, the respective rights and obligations with respect to intervention thresholds and deposit insurance.

References

Acharya, V., and M. Richardson, eds. 2009. *Restoring Financial Stability: How to Repair a Failed System*. Hoboken, NJ: Wiley Finance.

Acharya, V., and P. Schnabl. 2009. "How Banks Played the Leverage Game." In *Restoring Financial Stability: How to Repair a Failed System*, ed. V. Acharya and M. Richardson, pp. 83–100. Hoboken, NJ: Wiley Finance.

Adrian, T., and H. Shin. 2008. "Financial Intermediaries, Financial Stability, and Monetary Policy." Paper presented at symposium sponsored by the Federal Reserve of Kansas City, Jackson Hole, WY. Online at www.kc.frb.org/publicat/sympos/2008/Shin.08.06.08.pdf.

Aggarwal, R., and K. T. Jacques. 2001. "The Impact of FDICIA and Prompt Corrective Action on Bank Capital and Risk: Estimates Using a Simultaneous Equations Model." *Journal of Banking and Finance* 25: 1139–1160.

Aghion, P., P. Bolton, and S. Fries. 1999. "Optimal Design of Bank Bailouts: The Case of Transition Economies." *Journal of Institutional and Theoretical Economics* 155: 51–70.

Akerlof, G. 1970. "The Market for Lemons: Qualitative Uncertainty and the Market Mechanism." *Quarterly Journal of Economics* 84: 488–500.

Alexander, G., and A. Baptista. 2006. "Does the Basel Capital Accord Reduce Bank Fragility? An Assessment of the Value at Risk Approach." *Journal of Monetary Economics* 53: 1631–1660.

Allen, F., and D. Gale. 2005. "From Cash-in-the-Market Pricing to Financial Fragility." *Journal of the European Economic Association* 3: 535–546.

Anon. 2008. "Confessions of a Risk Manager." *Economist*, August 9, pp. 68–69.

Appelbaum, B., and E. Nakashima. 2008a. "Banking Regulator Played Advocate over Enforcer: Agency Let Lenders Grow Out of Control, Then Fail." *Washington Post*, November 23.

———. 2008b. "Regulator Let IndyMac Bank Falsify Report: Agency Didn't Enforce Its Rules, Inquiry Finds." *Washington Post*, December 23.

Ashcraft, A., and T. Schuermann. 2008. "Understanding the Securitization of Subprime Mortgage Credit." *Foundations and Trends in Finance* 2, no. 3: 191–309.

Asser, T.M.C. 2001. *Legal Aspects of Regulatory Treatment of Banks in Distress*. Washington, DC: International Monetary Fund.

Bank of France. 2007. *Financial Stability Review* (April). Special issue on hedge funds.

Basel Committee on Banking Supervision. 2009. Consultative Document: Proposed Enhancements to the Basel II Framework. Basel, January.

Bebchuk, L. 2009. "Toxic Tests." *Project Syndicate*, June. Online at www.project-syndicate.org/commentary/bebchuk2.

Bebchuk, L., and J. Fried. 2004. *Pay without Performance: The Unfulfilled Promise of Executive Compensation*. Cambridge, MA: Harvard University Press.

Bebchuk, L., and H. Spamann. Forthcoming. "Regulating Bankers' Pay." *Georgetown Law Journal*.

Benston, J. G., and G. J. Kaufman. 1997. "FDICIA after Five Years." *Journal of Economic Perspectives* 11: 139–158.

Bernanke, B. 2002. "Asset Price 'Bubbles' and Monetary Policy." Presentation to the New York Chapter of the National Association for Business Economics, New York, October 15. Online at www.federalreserve.gov/boarddocs/speeches/2002/20021015/default.htm.

———. 2009. "The Financial Crisis and Community Banking." Speech given at the Independent Community Bankers of America's National Convention and Techworld, Phoenix, March 20. Online at www.federalreserve.gov/newsevents/speech/bernanke20090320a.htm#fn3 68–9.

Blundell-Wignall, A., and P. Atkinson. 2008. "The Subprime Crisis: Causal Distortions and Regulatory Reforms." Discussion paper, Organization for Economic Cooperation and Development.

Blundell-Wignall, A., P. Atkinson, and S. H. Lee. 2008. "The Current Financial Crisis: Causes and Policy Issues." Organization for Economic Cooperation and Development, *Financial Market Trends*. Online at www.oecd.org/dataoecd/47/26/41942872.pdf.

Borio, C. 2003. *Towards a Macroprudential Framework for Financial Supervision and Regulation?* Basel: Bank for International Settlements.

Brunnermeier, M. 2009. "Deciphering the Liquidity and Credit Crunch, 2007–2008." *Journal of Economic Perspectives* 23, no. 1: 77–100.

Brunnermeier, M., A. Crockett, C. Goodhart, A. Persaud, and H. Shin. 2009. *The Fundamental Principles of Financial Regulation*. Geneva Report on the World Economy no. 11. London: Centre for Economic Policy Research.

Caballero, R. 2009. "A Global Perspective on the Great Financial Insurance Run: Causes, Consequences, and Solutions (Parts 1 and 2)." *Vox*, January 23. Online at www.voxeu.org/index.php?q=node/2828.

Caballero, R., E. Farhi, and P.-O. Gourinchas. 2008a. "An Equilibrium

Model of 'Global Imbalances' and Low Interest Rates." *American Economic Review* 98: 358–393.

———. 2008b. "Financial Crash, Commodity Prices and Global Imbalances." *Brookings Papers on Economic Activity* (fall): 1–55.

Caballero, R., and A. Simsek. 2009. "Complexity and Financial Panics." Working paper, MIT.

Calomiris, C. 2008. "The Subprime Turmoil: What's Old, What's New, What's Next." Paper presented at the ninth annual Jacques Polak Conference of the International Monetary Fund, November 13–14.

Calomiris, C., and C. Kahn. 1991. "The Role of Demandable Debt in Structuring Optimal Banking Arrangements." *American Economic Review* 81: 497–513.

Caruana, J. 2004. "Basel II: A New Approach to Banking Supervision." Remarks at the Fourth International Seminar on Policy Challenges for the Financial Sector, Washington, DC, June 1.

Commission Staff. 2008. European Commission Staff working document accompanying the "Proposal for a Regulation of the European Parliament and of the Council on Credit Rating Agencies."

Dash, E., and J. Creswell. 2008. "Citigroup Saw No Red Flags Even as It Made Bolder Bets." *New York Times*, November 23.

Davies, H. 2008. "Panel Comments." *Journal of Financial Stability* 4: 364–367.

de Larosière, J., et al. 2009. Report from the High-Level Group on Financial Supervision in the EU. Online at http://ec.europa.eu/internal_market/finances/docs/de_larosiere_report_en.pdf.

De Soto, H. 2000. *The Mystery of Capital: Why Capitalism Triumphs in the West and Fails Everywhere Else*. New York: Basic Books.

Dewatripont, M., I. Jewitt, and J. Tirole. 1999. "The Economics of Career Concerns, Part II: Application to Missions and Accountability of Government Agencies." *Review of Economic Studies* 66: 199–217.

Dewatripont, M., and J. Tirole. 1994. *The Prudential Regulation of Banks*. Cambridge, MA: MIT Press.

Diamond, D., and P. Dybvig. 1983. "Bank Runs, Deposit Insurance, and Liquidity." *Journal of Political Economy* 91: 401–419.

Diamond, D., and R. Rajan. 2001. "Liquidy Risk, Liquidy Creation, and Financial Fragility: A Theory of Banking." *Journal of Political Economy* 109: 287–327.

Dierick, F., F. Pires, M. Scheicher, and K. G. Spitzer. 2005. "The New Basel Capital Framework and Its Implementation in the European Union." European Central Bank Discussion Paper no. 42, December.

Farhi, E., and J. Tirole. 2009. "Collective Moral Hazard, Maturity Mismatch, and Systemic Bailouts." Working paper, Harvard University and Toulouse Sciences Economiques.

———. 2010. "Bubbly Liquidity." Working paper, Harvard University and Toulouse Sciences Economiques.

Faure-Grimaud, A. 2002. "Using Stock Price Information to Regulate Firms." *Review of Economic Studies* 69: 169–180.

Fender, I., and J. Mitchell. 2009. "Incentives and Tranche Retention in Securitisation: A Screening Model." Working paper, Bank for International Settlements, National Bank of Belgium, and CEPR.

Financial Stability Forum. 2009. "FSF Principles for Sound Compensation Practices." April 2.

Franke, G., and J. P. Krahnen. 2008. "The Future of Securitization." Working Paper no. 31, Centre for Financial Studies, Frankfurt a.M.

Freixas, X. 2003. "Crisis Management in Europe." In *Financial Supervision in Europe*, ed. J. Kremers, D. Schoenmaker, and P. Wierts, pp. 129–138. Cheltenham: Edward Elgar.

Freixas, X., and B. M. Parigi. 2008. "Banking Regulation and Prompt Corrective Action." Paper presented at the 21st Australasian Finance and Banking Conference, 2008. Available at http://ssrn.com/abstract =1153447.

Freixas, X., and J.-C. Rochet. 2008. *Microeconomics of Banking*, 2nd ed. Cambridge, MA: MIT Press.

Goodhart, C. 2008. "The Regulatory Response to the Financial Crisis." *Journal of Financial Stability* 4: 351–358.

Gordy, M. 2003. "A Risk-Factor Model Foundation for Ratings-Based Bank Capital Rules." *Journal of Financial Intermediation* 12, no. 3: 199–232.

Group of Thirty. 2009. "Financial Reform: A Framework for Financial Stability." Online at www.group30.org/pubs/recommendations .pdf.

Hellwig, M. 2009. "Systemic Risk in the Financial Sector: An Analysis of the Subprime-Mortgage Financial Crisis." *De Economist* 157: 129–207.

Herring, R. 2006. "Conflicts between Home and Host Country Prudential Supervisors." Working paper, University of Pennsylvania. Online at http://fic.wharton.upenn.edu/fic/papers/07/0733.pdf.

Holmström, B. 1979. "Moral Hazard and Observability." *Bell Journal of Economics* 10: 74–91.

———. 2008. Discussion of Gary Gorton, "The Panic of 2007." Paper presented at symposium sponsored by the Federal Reserve of Kansas City, Jackson Hole, WY. Online at http://econ-www.mit.edu/files/ 3784.

Holmström, B., and J. Tirole. 1997. "Financial Intermediation, Loanable Funds, and the Real Sector." *Quarterly Journal of Economics* 112: 663–692.

————. 1998. "Private and Public Supply of Liquidity." *Journal of Political Economy* 106: 1–40.

Hoshi, T., and A. Kashyap. 2008. "Will the TARP Succeed? Lessons from Japan." NBER Working Paper no. 14401, National Bureau of Economic Research.

Institute of International Finance. 2008. "Financial Services Industry Response to the Market Turmoil of 2007–2008." Washington, DC.

International Monetary Fund. 2008. *Global Financial Stability Report.* Washington, DC: International Monetary Fund, October.

Jackson, P., C. Furfine, H. Groeneveld, D. Hancock, D. Jones, W. Perraudin, L. Radecki, and M. Yoneyama. 1999. "Capital Requirements and Bank Behaviour: The Impact of the Basle Accord." Basle Committee on Banking Supervision Working Papers no. 1, April.

Kashyap, A., R. G. Rajan, and J. C. Stein. 2008. "Rethinking Capital Regulation." Working paper.

Kashyap, A., and J. Stein. 2003. "Cyclical Implications of the Basel II Capital Standards." Discussion paper, University of Chicago Graduate School of Business.

Keys, B., T. Mukherjee, A. Seru, and V. Vig. Forthcoming. "Did Securitization Lead to Lax Screening? Evidence from Subprime Loans." *Quarterly Journal of Economics* 125, no. 1.

Kindleberger, C. P. 2000. *Manias, Panics, and Crashes: A History of Financial Crises.* New York: Wiley.

Kovbasyuk, S. 2010. "Optimal Certification Design." Mimeo, Toulouse School of Economics.

Krimminger, M. H. 2008. "The Resolution of Cross-Border Banks: Issues for Deposit Insurers and Proposals for Cooperation." *Journal of Financial Stability* 4: 376–390.

Labaton, S. 2008. "Agency's '04 Rule Lets Banks Pile Up New Debt." *New York Times,* October 2.

Lannoo, K. 2008. "Concrete Steps towards More Integrated Financial Oversight: The EU's Policy Response to the Crisis." CEPS Task Force Report, Centre for European Policy Studies.

Lorenzoni, G. 2008. "Inefficient Credit Booms." *Review of Economic Studies* 75: 809–833.

Lowenstein, R. 2000. *When Genius Failed: The Rise and Fall of LTCM.* New York: Random House.

Matherat, S. 2008. "Fair Value Accounting and Financial Stability: Challenges and Dynamics." Bank of France, *Financial Stability Review* 12 (October): 53–63.

Mathis, J., J. McAndrews, and J.-C. Rochet. 2009. "Rating the Raters: Are Reputation Concerns Powerful Enough to Discipline Rating Agencies?" *Journal of Monetary Economics* 56: 657–674.

Mitchell, J. 2001. "Bad Debts and the Cleaning of Banks' Balance Sheets: An Application to Economies in Transition." *Journal of Financial Intermediation* 10: 1–27.

Praet, P., and P. Nguyen. 2008. "Overview of Recent Policy Initiatives in Response to the Crisis." *Journal of Financial Stability* 4: 368–375.

Rebonato, R. 2007. *The Plight of the Fortune Tellers: Why We Need to Manage Financial Risk Differently*. Princeton, NJ: Princeton University Press.

Rochet, J.-C. 2004. "Macroeconomic Shocks and Banking Supervision." *Journal of Financial Stability* 1: 93–110. Reprinted in Rochet (2008b).

———. 2008a. "Procyclicality of Financial Systems: Is There a Need to Modify Current Accounting and Regulatory Rules?" Bank of France, *Financial Stability Review* 12 (October): 95–99.

———. 2008b. *Why Are There So Many Banking Crises? The Politics and Policy of Bank Regulation*. Princeton, NJ: Princeton University Press.

Rochet, J. C., and J. Tirole. 1996. "Controlling Risk in Payment Systems." *Journal of Money, Credit, and Banking* 28: 832–862.

Saurina, J., and C. Trucharte. 2007. "An Assessment of Basel II Procyclicality in Mortgage Portfolios." Bank of Spain Working Paper no. 0712, July.

Schoenmaker, D., and C. Goodhart. 2006. "Burden Sharing in a Banking Crisis in Europe." FMG Special Papers no. sp164.

Shiller, R. 2009. *The Subprime Solution*. Princeton, NJ: Princeton University Press.

Suarez, J. 2008. "The Need for an Emergency Bank Debt Insurance Mechanism." CEPR Policy Insight no. 19, Centre for Economic Policy Research.

Tarullo, D. 2008. *Banking on Basel: The Future of International Financial Regulation*. Washington, DC: Peterson Institute for International Economics.

Taylor, A., and C. Goodhart. 2004. "Procyclicality and Volatility in the Financial System: The Implementation of Basel II and IAS 39." Working paper, Financial Markets Group, London School of Economics.

Tett, G. 2009. *Fool's Gold: How the Bold Dream of a Small Tribe at J. P. Morgan Was Corrupted by Wall Street Greed and Unleashed a Catastrophe*. New York: Free Press.

Tirole, J. 2002. *Financial Crises, Liquidity, and the International Monetary System*. Princeton, NJ: Princeton University Press.

van de Woestyne, F., and A. van Caloen. 2009. *Fortis, Dexia . . . le Séisme*. Brussels: Ed. Luc Pire.

Wilson, J. Q. 1989. *Bureaucracy: What Government Agencies Do and Why They Do It*. New York: Basic Books.

Index